HISTORICAL BOOKS

VERY REV. PETER SAMUEL KUCER, MSA

En Route Books and Media, LLC
St. Louis, MO

En Route Books and Media, LLC
5705 Rhodes Avenue
St. Louis, MO 63109

Cover credit: TJ Burdick

Library of Congress Control Number: 2020944372

ISBN-13: 978-1-952464-27-0

Acknowledgements

I would particularly like to acknowledge Very Rev. Edward Przygocki, M.S.A., U.S.A., Province Provincial of the Missionaries of the Holy Apostles, who gave me permission to publish.

Special thanks also to Dr. Sebastian Mahfood, O.P., President of En Route Books and Media, for publishing this work.

Contents

Introduction

In a private revelation, Mechthild of Magdeburg heard the Lord say, "One should never ordain anyone a priest unless he is familiar with both the Old and the New Testament, because with just one leg no one can go to court or serve for any length of time."[1] Hopefully, these brief chapters on the historical books of the Old Testament will be a way by which all, especially those aspiring to the priesthood, can become familiar with the Old Testament. In striving for this goal, these chapters on the various historical books will introduce the reader to various spiritual ways of interpreting the text.

In accordance with the *Catechism of the Catholic Church*'s definition of authentic, spiritual interpretations of Scripture, the presented spiritual interpretations will be grounded in the literal, historical meaning intended by the inspired author. The spiritual meaning represents the meaning that God, as primary author, includes within the literal, historical meaning and which transcends the historical meaning without contradicting it.[2] The *Catechism* divides

---

[1] Mechthild of Magdeburg, *The Flowing Light of the Godhead*, trans. Frank Tobin (New York: Paulist Press, 1998), loc. 2507.

[2] A proper literal interpretation will take into account the literary form of the writing that is being interpreted. If the literary form is not acknowledged when interpreting the passage, the interpretation will often err by being overly literalistic since it does not take into account the form of the writing. A literary form indicates if a passage is intended to be interpreted

the spiritual interpretation in three ways: moral, pertaining to heaven (anagogical), and fulfilled by a higher reality (allegorical).[3]

The three-fold spiritual interpretation of Scripture can also be described as a theological interpretation since the word theology literally means words on God. The spiritual interpretation brings to the fore, in the words of Benedict XVI, the "one voice of the whole" of Scripture who is God as primary author who speaks through Scripture to all in every time. This theological interpretation ("theological exegesis"), adds Benedict XVI, "seek[s] the inner identity" who is God as primary author. As the primary author of Scripture, as the primary voice of Scripture, God "sustains the whole" of Scripture with its many human authors "and binds it together."[4]

The "three criteria" for interpreting Scripture, whether literally or spiritually are, the *Catechism* states, "the content and unity of the whole Scripture…the living Tradition of the whole Church…[and] the analogy of faith."[5] In simpler language these three criteria correspond

---

as an historical narrative or is to be interpreted symbolically. Various literary forms listed by Scott Hahn are "a narrative, a poem, a letter, a parable, or an apocalyptic vision." *Ignatius Catholic Study Bible, Joshua, Commentary, Notes, & Study Questions, Revised Standard Version, Second Catholic Edition, with Introduction, Commentary, and Notes by Scott Hahn, and Curtis Mitch* (San Francisco: Ignatius Press, 2016), kindle location 95.

[3] "Catechism of the Catholic Church, no. 117" vatican.va, http://www.vatican.va/archive/ccc_css/archive/catechism/p1s1c2a3.htm.

[4] Joseph Ratzinger, and Hans Urs von Balthasar, *Mary, the Church at the Source*, trans. A. Walker (San Francisco: Ignatius Press, 2005) 39.

[5] "Catechism of the Catholic Church, no. 113-114," vatican.va, http://www.vatican.va/archive/ENG0015/__PQ.HTM#$3B . The *Catechism* cites *Dei Verbum* chapter 3, no. 12.

to first interpreting a specific passage of Scripture in light of Scripture as a whole with the belief that God as primary author does not contradict Himself. Second, Scriptural interpretation is to be done in light of living Tradition which consists in how the Holy Spirit has directed and inspired the Church, Fathers, Doctors, and saints. Finally, interpreting Scripture is to be done by allowing the various beliefs of our faith, as defined by the Magisterium the official teaching office of the Church, interpret one another in a similar manner as Scripture interprets Scripture since its author is one, God.[6]

[6] *Ignatius Catholic Study Bible, Joshua, Commentary, Notes, & Study Questions,* Kindle location 187.

Joshua

Introduction

The first historical book is Joshua. When reading Joshua, John Bergsma and Brant Pitre note the following two points. First, it is important to keep in mind that the use of hyperbole, in which events are narrated in an exaggerated manner, was common during ancient times and such exaggerations would have been easily identified by ancient readers. When this is remembered, then a contradiction between two or more passages that describe the same event may simply be due to one description being an exaggerated narrative.

Secondly, as in modern day warfare, simply because one nation defeats another in battle does not mean that the additional warfare is no longer needed. Often further smaller battles are needed in order to further subdue the population in taking full control of the land. According to this distinction, therefore, just because an early passage of Joshua claims that the Israelites defeated its enemies in battle while a latter passage describes additional skirmishes between the Israelites and the people of the land does not mean these passages contradiction one another and is sufficient evidence for arguing that Joshua is comprised of a number of competing and, at times, contradictory sources.[1]

---

[1] John Bergsma and Brant Pitre, *A Catholic Introduction to the Bible, Volume I* (San Francisco: Ignatius Press, 2018), 299-301.

With that said, it is possible, as some Scripture scholars contend, that there were multiple sources that were brought together to form Joshua. A Catholic spiritual reading of the book of Joshua, though, will focus less on the secondary author, in particular Joshua, (Joshua 8:32; 24:26) or authors of Joshua and more on the principle author who is God. We now turn our attention to the following people and features of this inspired book to hear what spiritual messages God is speaking through the book. First, we will focus on two people: Joshua and Rahab. Then, we will shift our attention to Jericho, herem warfare, and end with cities of refuge.

[2]

[2] Jewish Museum [Public domain], "The Ark Passes Over the Jordan (watercolor circa 1896–1902 by James Tissot)," https://commons.wikimedia.org/wiki/File:James_Jacques_Joseph_Tissot_-_The_Ark_Passes_Over_the_Jordan_-_Google_Art_Project.jpg.

Joshua

The principle person of Joshua is present in the Pentateuch first as "Hoshea the son of Nun" (Numbers 13:8 RSV). A few verses later, Moses selects Hoshea along with eleven other men to spy on the Canaanites and then changes Hoshea name to Joshua (Numbers 13:16). The Hebrew name Hoshea (הוֹשֵׁעַ) means salvation. A number of Israelite men in the Pentateuch and in the Historical Books share this Hebrew name.[3] The Hebrew name that Hoshea the son of Nun is changed to is *Yehoshua* (יְהוֹשׁוּעַ), which the English name Joshua comes from. The Hebrew name for Joshua, Yehoshua, is a made up by two Hebrew words, *YHWH* (יְהוָה), the proper name of God with the vowels from Adonai, and *yasha* (יָשַׁע) the root for deliver.[4] The compound word name, Yehoshua (Joshua in English) literally means, therefore, God is salvation, or God saves.

In English the name Yehoshua is translated either as Joshua or Jesus. These two names, therefore, are equivalent. Church Fathers picked up this equivalence and interpreted Jesus as a new Joshua and Joshua as foreshadowing Jesus as a type with Jesus as the fulfillment of Joshua. According to John Chrysostom (347-407), the deeper reason why Joshua's name was changed by Moses was to indicate his different mission from Moses'.

Although Moses' mission was to teach people in the requirements

---

3 "1954. Hoshea," Strong's Concordance, biblehub.com, https://biblehub.com/hebrew/1954.htm .

4 "3068. Yhvh," Strong's Concordance, biblehub.com, https://biblehub.com/hebrew/3068.htm; "3467. Yasha," Strong's Concordance, biblehub.com, https://biblehub.com/hebrew/3467.htm .

of the law, in the requirements of Torah (תּוֹרָה) (meaning teaching, instruction, and law), he still died outside of the Promised Land thereby teaching that the law by itself has no power to save, has no power to bring a person into the Promised Land. In contrast, the mission of Joshua, whose very name God saves, entered the promised land and lead other people into the land not because of any merit of his own, or because of the law but because of grace, because of the gift of salvation from God who saves.[5]

In fulfillment of Joshua's role who was only a man, Jesus as the God man, as the new Joshua truly offers us salvation, truly offers us the Promised Land of Heaven. We only can receive this gift if we freely accept the Sanctifying Grace he offers and pray for the grace to persevere in this gift of salvation, in the gift of Sanctifying Grace so as to cross over the waters of death to reach Jesus who is heaven as Pope Benedict XVI states, "Jesus himself is what we call 'heaven', heaven is not a place but a person, the person of him in whom God and man are forever and inseparably one. And we go to heaven and enter into heaven to the extent that we go to Jesus Christ and enter into him."[6]

Finally, Jesus as the one who leads us into the Promised Land in its fullest sense and as the Promised Land in person also fulfills Joshua's role in yet another important way. Under Moses' leadership the Israelites wandered through the desert, eating heavenly manna with the hope to reach the Promised Land. Joshua, then, leads the Israelites

---

[5] John R. Franke, *Ancient Christian Commentary on Scripture: Old Testament IV, Joshua, Judges, Ruth, 1-2 Samuel* (Downers Grove: Intervarsity Press, 2014), 3.

[6] Benedict XVI, *Day by Day with Pope Benedict XVI*, ed. Peter John Cameron (San Francisco: Ignatius Press, 2006), 153.

across the Jordan River and in so doing the manna from heaven ceases to appear since the Israelites have reached the Promised Land of plenty and are no longer in a desert. After the example of the Church Fathers, Hahn implies that Jesus fulfills the role of the manna in the desert by his Eucharistic presence which is the heavenly manna for Catholics as we make a pilgrimage through this world to the heavenly Promised Land. In heaven, the manna, and the entire sacramental system will give way to what they signify, or rather who they signify, Jesus, Jesus head and members, including the saints of heaven as members of His body.[7]

Section Questions

1. What does the name Joshua mean in Hebrew and how is it related to the name Jesus?

Rahab

Before leading his people over the Jordan River into the Promised Land, Joshua sent two Israelite men to spy on the city of Jericho. The spies stayed in the home of Rahab, a prostitute. When Rahab was commanded by her king to "Bring forth the men that have come to you, who entered your house (Joshua 2:3 *RSVCE*)" she claims that they left, and she does not know where they went. In reality, she had hidden

---

[7] *Ignatius Catholic Study Bible, Joshua, Commentary, Notes, & Study Questions, Revised Standard Version, Second Catholic Edition, with Introduction, Commentary, and Notes by Scott Hahn, and Curtis Mitch* (San Francisco: Ignatius Press, 2016), kindle location 1511.

the two Israelites on the roof of her house. In gratitude, the spies assure Rahab that if she gathers her family together in her house, ties a "scarlet cord" to a window of her house, the Israelites will spare her life and her family's lives. Rahab heeds their request, and the Israelites make sure she and her family are not harmed. In Jesus' genealogy of Matthew's Gospel, Rahab is listed as having married Salmon, the great-great-grandfather of King David (Matthew 1:5).

[8]

The Church Fathers interpreted Rahab as a type of the Church. According to Gregory Baeticus of Elvira (c. d. 392 A.D.), even though Rahab was a prostitute:

[8] Julius Schnorr von Carolsfeld [Public domain], "Rahab lets the spies escape in this 1860 woodcut by Julius Schnorr von Karolsfeld," https://commons.wikimedia.org/wiki/File:Schnorr_von_Carolsfeld_Bibel_in_Bildern_1860_066.png.

> nevertheless [she] is a sign of the virgin Church, considered as a foreshadow of the coming realities at the end of the age, where she alone is preserved to life among all who are perishing ... Indeed, she is called "the church" because the Greek word *ecclesia* means "gathering of the people." And just as [St Paul] says, "An unfaithful wife is sanctified through her faithful husband," so also is the church, coming from the infidelity of the Gentiles and prostitution with idols, sanctified through the body of Christ, of which we are members, as we learn from [St Paul].[9]

Rahab's welcoming, sheltering, hiding, and sending out two Israelite spies by a rope through the window of her home is interpreted by Cassiodorus (c. 490-583) as "a type of the church, which takes in souls endangered by the vice of pride, and lets them out into life by another route, the way of humility and patience."[10] Cyprian of Carthage (c. 200-258 A.D.) describes Rahab gathering her family together under the one roof of her house as an important detail of her role as a type of the Church. This action foreshadows the Catholic Church for "all who are to live and escape the destruction of the world must be gathered into one house alone, the Church."[11] According to the Magisterium, one may be gathered into the saving house of the Church by the ordinary way of Baptism and by desire, even unconscious desire,: "Every man who is ignorant of the Gospel of Christ and his Church, but seeks the truth and does the will of God in

---

[9] Franke, 9.

[10] Franke, 9.

[11] Franke, 14.

accordance with his understanding of it, can be save. It may be supposed that such persons would have *desired Baptism explicitly* if they had known its necessity (*CCC* 1261)."[12]

In the quoted verse by Cyprian, the scarlet cloth that Rahab is told to hang outside of her window is identified as fulfilled by the blood of Christ. In the book of Joshua, the red cloth signaled to the conquering Israelites to spare Rahab and her family. The New Testament's blood of Christ fulfills this by offering salvation from eternal death.

Section Questions

1. Who did Rahab marry and how is her husband specifically related to Jesus?

2. As stated in the lectures, describe in one specific way how Church Fathers understood Rahab as a type of Jesus and His Church.

Jericho

The Israelite conquering of Rahab's city of Jericho has been spiritually interpreted in a variety of ways. Joshua's careful planning of the attack by sending spies into the city represents, Hamilton interprets, the collaborative dimension of Divine Providence. Even though God promised Joshua that he would be aided by God as Moses was, this promise did not nullify "human responsibility" writes

---

[12] "Catechism of the Catholic Church, no. 1261," vatican.va, http://www.vatican.va/archive/ccc_css/archive/catechism/p2s2c1a1.htm .

Hamilton, instead the promises are brought about in a collaborative manner "along the lines of 'faith without works is dead.'"[13]

Gregory of Nyssa (c.335-c.395 A.D.) interprets both what Joshua and the Israelites left behind when crossing the Jordan river and what they encountered and destroyed as representing sin:

> Imitate Joshua, the son of Nun. Carry the Gospel as he carried the Ark. Leave the desert, that is to say, sin. Cross the Jordan. Hasten toward life according to Christ, toward the earth that bears the fruits of joy, where run, according to the promise, streams of milk and honey. Overthrow Jericho, the old dwelling-place, do not leave it fortified. All these things are a figure [*typos*] of ourselves. All are pre-figurations of realities that now are made manifest.[14]

The twelve stones that God commanded Joshua to take out of the Jordan river, "according to the number of the tribes" and place on the west bank of the Jordan are interpreted by Church Fathers in reference to Christ's mission. In addition to these stones, Joshua also placed another set of twelve stones "in the midst of the Jordan, in the place where the feet of the priests bearing the ark of the covenant had stood (Joshua 4:9 RSV)." In interpreting the latter set of stones, Gregory of Nyssa asserts, "it is clear that Joshua also, who set up the twelve stones

---

[13] Victor P. Hamilton, *Handbook on the Historical Books* (Grand Rapids: Baker Publishing Group, 2001), 28.

[14] Adrien Nocent, *The Liturgical Year: Advent, Christmas, Epiphany, Volume 1*, (Collegeville: Liturgical Press, 2013), 240. Nocent cites "Daniélou, *The Bible and the Liturgy*, 102-103."

in the stream [the Jordan River], was anticipating the coming of the twelve disciples, the ministers of baptism."[15]

[16]

[15] Franke, 20.

[16] James Tissot [Public domain], "The Taking of Jericho (watercolor circa 1896–1902 by James Tissot)," https://commons.wikimedia.org/wiki/File:Tissot_The_Taking_of_Jericho.jpg.

Reflection on the way the Israelites defeated and destroyed Jericho after crossing the Jordan has yielded a variety of interpretations. Maximus of Turin interpreted the destruction of Jericho as a symbol of Christ's coming at the end of time when "the heavens will pass away with a loud noise, and the elements will be dissolved with fire, and the earth and the works that are upon it will be burned up (2 Peter 3:10 *RSVCE*)" and what remains will be transformed into "new heavens and a new earth (2 Peter 3:13 *RSVCE*)."[17]

Maximus highlights the seven days that God commanded the Israelites to march around the city of Jericho following seven priests blowing rams' horns as a judgement on the entire world that was created in seven days and afterwards sank into sin. Similarly, St. Paul teaches that the end of the world will come after Christ returns "from heaven…and with the sound of the trumpet of God (1 Thessalonians 4:16 *RSVCE*)."[18] Both judgments, the judgment of Jericho and the judgment at the end of time, are followed by destruction that takes place within a liturgical context in which God directly intervenes in history. The destruction of evil, represented by Jericho's demise, and the triumph of good does not take place primarily because of man's military might and cunning but is rather an action that is essentially a divine act that invites the participation of human action. Reflecting this understanding, St. Augustine writes:

> So the walls of that city, called Jericho…fell when they had been encircled seven times by the ark of the covenant. What, then, does the announcement of the kingdom of heaven portend—

[17] Franke, 36.

[18] Franke, 36.

> signified by the encircling of the ark—except that all the battlements of mortal life, that is, all the hope of this world, which is opposed to the hope of the world to come, will be destroyed by the sevenfold gift of the Holy Spirit, working through the free will? For, those walls fell of their own accord, not by any violent push of the ark in its circuit.

Like Augustine, Dom Scupoli in *The Spiritual Combat* teaches that doing good, avoiding evil and growing in holiness is to take place within the context of collaboration between God and human beings. Scupoli writes:

> Since, therefore, you seek the highest degree of perfection, you must wage continual warfare against yourself and employ your entire strength in demolishing each vicious inclination, however trivial. … It is true, considering things in themselves, that the conversion of a soul is, without doubt, infinitely more acceptable to the Divine Majesty than the mortification of a disorderly affection. Yet, every person, in his own particular sphere, should begin with what is immediately required of him. … Now that you know what Christian perfection is and that, in order to attain it, you must resolve on a perpetual warfare with yourself, begin by providing yourself with four weapons without which it is impossible to gain the victory in this spiritual combat: distrust of one's self, confidence in God, proper use of the faculties of body and mind, and the duty of

> prayer.[19]

At first, it may appear that Scupoli is stressing human effort more than God's grace. However, a more careful look indicates that the emphasis is not on human effort but on reliance on God as the last few lines of the quoted passage make explicit. Three of the four "weapons" used to be victorious in spiritual combat are all ways of relying on God and his strength while relying less on one's own efforts, "distrust of one's self, confidence in God" and "prayer". The third "weapon" is "proper use of the faculties of body and mind" which only can take place if trust is placed primarily in God by acknowledging that victory is essentially a gift of God in a similar way as victory for the Israelites over Jericho was primarily, writes Hahn, "a 'gift' that God is giving to Israel; only secondarily is it something to be taken by conquest."[20]

Section Questions

1. As stated in the lectures, describe in one specific way how Church Fathers or more modern commentators interpreted the Israelite seven-day march around Jericho.

---

[19] Dom Lorenzo Scupoli, *The Spiritual Combat*, trans. William Lester and Robert Paul Mohan (Catholic Way Publishing, 2013), Kindle Location 102-111.

[20] *Ignatius Catholic Study Bible, Joshua, Commentary, Notes, & Study Questions,* kindle location 1357.

Herem Warfare

According to Joshua, the city of Jericho, "and all that is within it shall be devoted to the Lord for destruction (Joshua 6:17 RSV)." The Hebrew word used to for devoting something to God in a total manner is *herem* (חֵרֶם). *Herem* is based on the Hebrew root *charam* (חָרַם) meaning both devotion and destruction, such as when Jericho was destroyed.[21]

[22]

[21] "Strong's Concordance, 2763. charam," biblehub.com, https://biblehub.com/hebrew/2763.htm.

[22] Gustave Doré [Public domain], "Gustave Doré, The Death of Agag. Agag was executed by Samuel as part of God's command to put the

As pointed out by Bergsma and Pitre, presenting the destruction of Jericho as part of a Holy War can be misleading since the Hebrew language, and consequently the Old Testament, does not have this terminology. Instead, when the bible refers to the total destruction of cities it uses the term referred to above, *herem* (חֶרֶם). *Herem* is used to describe something that is completely given to God. For example, Leviticus uses the term in reference to a field that is set aside for God and the priests (Leviticus 27:21), and Ezekiel uses the same term for what has been set aside for God, including cereal offerings (Ezekiel 44:29). Later, this same chapter describes something that has been totally set aside and, consequently, "is most holy to the Lord (Leviticus 27:28 *RSVCE*)." *Herem* objects that are devoutly offered to God are also at times to destroyed in the process. For this reason, Jericho was only destroyed after the Israelites solemnly followed priests blowing rams' horns as they marched around the city of Jericho.[23]

When interpreting the total destruction of Jericho and other cities in the Bible we can build upon the inherent spiritual reason of devoting something totally to God that a *herem* object implies. As cited by Bergsma and Pitre, the mystic St. John of the Cross refers to *herem* with, "The lesson here is that all objects living in the soul—whether they be many or few, large or small—must die in order that the soul enter divine union, and it must bear no desire for them but remain detached as though they were nonexistent to it, and it to them."[24] This New Testament spiritual interpretation of Old Testament passages

Amalekites under herem (1 Samuel 15)," https://commons.wikimedia.org/wiki/File:Gustave_Dor%C3%A9_Morte_Agag.jpg.

[23] Bergsma and Pitre, 305.

[24] Bergsma and Pitre, 314.

that appear highly troubling helps to resolve the difficulty by deemphasizing what was destroyed, including women and children which is deeply troubling, while focusing more on the principle of devoting something, or someone to God in a total sense. John of the Cross does so by using the practice of *herem* as supportive of the basic spiritual principle that growing in spiritual perfection entails completely ending disordered attachments to created reality and, in so doing, order all these attachments in a right relationship to God.[25]

Similar to John of the Cross's mystical interpretation, Origin applies God commanding the Israelites to destroy their enemies as given ultimate meaning in Jesus in relationship to each person's struggle to conquer their evil tendencies:

> [The Israelites] are ordered to trample upon the necks of their enemies and to suspend from wood the kings of that land that they violently invade. And yet, if only my Lord Jesus the Son of God would grant that to me and order me to crush the spirit of fornication with my feet and trample upon the necks of the spirit of wrath and rage, to trample on the demon of avarice, to trample down boasting, to crush the spirit of arrogance with my feet, and, when I have done all these things, not to hang the most exalted of these exploits upon myself, but upon his cross. Thereby I imitate Paul, who says, "the world is crucified to me," and, that which we have already related above, "Not I, but the grace of God that is in me."[26]

---

[25] Bergsma and Pitre, 314.

[26] Franke, 62.

Applying these passages on the Israelite destruction of cities to Jesus's desire for each disciple to cooperate with His grace so as to experience victory over sinful tendencies is also reflected in Augustine's writing on two cities, Jerusalem and Babylon, which represent two civilizations, Jerusalem, representing a peaceful, loving, life-centered city ordered around worship of God and Babylon, symbolizing a violent, disordered, excessively competitive city ordered by worship of self. The struggle of these two civilizations for dominance takes place in the heart of every human being. In writing on how these two civilizations of life and death relate St. Augustine describes them "mingled, and from the very beginning of humankind mingled they run on until the end of the world. Jerusalem began through Abel, Babylon through Cain: ... and to remain even until the end in this world, but at the end to be severed."[27]

In addition to a spiritual interpretation of *herem*, Bergsma and Pitre provide other reasons including, "*The Divine Pedagogy Explanation*" where these passages are placed in the context of the gradual unfolding of revelation that, according to Matthew J. Ramage, "record for us what [the Israelites] *thought* God wanted them to carry out rather than what he has *actually* willed."[28] Benedict XVI in his Apostolic Exhortation *Verbum Domini* describes the gradual unfolding of revelation leading up to the fullness of revelation in Jesus Christ with:

> [I]t must be remembered first and foremost that *biblical revelation is deeply rooted in history.* God's plan is

---

[27] Franke, 86.

[28] Bergsma and Pitre, 307.

manifested *progressively* and it is accomplished slowly, *in successive stages* and despite human resistance. God chose a people and patiently worked to guide and educate them. Revelation is suited to the cultural and moral level of distant times and thus describes facts and customs, such as cheating and trickery, and acts of violence and massacre, without explicitly denouncing the immorality of such things. This can be explained by the historical context, yet it can cause the modern reader to be taken aback, especially if he or she fails to take account of the many "dark" deeds carried out down the centuries, and also in our own day. In the Old Testament, the preaching of the prophets vigorously challenged every kind of injustice and violence, whether collective or individual, and thus became God's way of training his people in preparation for the Gospel. So it would be a mistake to neglect those passages of Scripture that strike us as problematic. Rather, we should be aware that the correct interpretation of these passages requires a degree of expertise, acquired through a training that interprets the texts in their historical-literary context and within the Christian perspective which has as its ultimate hermeneutical key "the Gospel and the new commandment of Jesus Christ brought about in the paschal mystery." I encourage scholars and pastors to help all the faithful to approach these passages through an interpretation which enables their meaning to emerge in the light of the mystery of Christ.[29]

---

[29] Benedict XVI, "Post-Synodal Apostolic Exhortation Verbum Domini, 2010," W2.vatican.va, http://w2.vatican.va/content/benedict-xvi/en/apost_

Two additional explanations provided by Bergsma and Pitre for these "dark" passages of Scripture are "The Divine Judgment Explanation" and "The Deuteronomic Concession Explanation."[30] According to the Divine Judgment Explanation, which Thomas Aquinas held, explain Bergsma and Pitre, "insofar as man has merited man has merited physical death through original sin, God cannot be charged with injustice when he takes the life of anyone, even those innocent of actual sin, such as children."[31]

According to the Deuteronomic Concession Explanation "scholars have emphasized that, from a salvation-historical point of view, the command to pursue *herem* warfare against the cities of Canaanites in the land is not part of the original Sinai covenant, but a concession to Israel's sinfulness and hard-heartedness."[32] Hahn cites Ezekiel's reference to bad laws given by God to the Israelites as supportive of this explanation. In Ezekiel chapter twenty, God tells Ezekiel, "Moreover I gave them statutes that were not good and ordinances by which they could not have life (Ezekiel 20:25 *RSVCE*)."[33]

In reference to Hahn, Bergsma writes, "This holy war was a concession of the Deuteronomic covenant, announced after the Israelites had twice lapsed into idolatrous worship during the wilderness period; its stern provisions were necessary because God

---

exhortations/documents/hf_ben-xvi_exh_20100930_verbum-domini.html, no. 42.

[30] Bergsma and Pitre, 308-310.

[31] Bergsma and Pitre, 309.

[32] Bergsma and Pitre, 309.

[33] *Ignatius Catholic Study Bible, Joshua, Commentary, Notes, & Study Questions,* kindle location 1603.

knew that otherwise his people were too weak to resist the attraction of Canaanite idolatry."[1] To demonstrate this Bergsma and Pitre provide the following chart:

Historical Context	***Command to Israelites***
Mount Sinai:	Be a "kingdom of priests". (Ex 19:5-6)
Post-Golden Calf:	Destroy altars of Canaanites and make no covenant with them. (Ex. 34:11-16)
Post-Apostasy at Moab:	Destroy altars and drive out the Canaanites from the land. (Num 33:50-56)
Final Speech of Moses:	Utterly destroy the Canaanites in the land, as well as any Israelite city that becomes idolatrous. (Deut 7:1-11; 12:29031; 20:10-18; cf. Deut. 13:12-18)

[34]

Section Questions

1. Fill in the blank. *Herem* is based on the Hebrew root *charam* (חָרַם) meaning both _________ and _____________.

2. How does St. John of the Cross spiritually interpret the Hebrew concept of a *herem* object, like Jericho?

3. How does Matthew J. Ramage explain herem warfare? Include

---

[34] Bergsma and Pitre, 305-310.

in your answer the following: Gradual, God's Actual Will, Stages of Revelation, Fulness of Revelation.

4. How does Scott Hahn explain herem warfare according to concessionary law? Include the following in your answer: Mount Sinai, Post-Golden Calf, Post-Apostasy at Moab, Final Speech of Moses.

Cities of Refuge

After conquering the Canaanite cities, Joshua assigns land to specific tribes, except for the tribe of Levi since as the tribe of priests "the Lord God of Israel is their inheritance (Joshua 13:33 RSV)." This tribe of priests is, though, tasked with the responsibilities to oversee six cities of refuge (Numbers 35:1-15; Joshua 21). Cities of refuge were safe places that someone who had committed unintentional manslaughter could flee to and remain safe from those seeking vengeance.

Church Fathers interpreted these sanctuary cities as fulfilled in Christ and in a specific manner by Christ's presence in Baptism and the Sacrament of Confession. Those seeking refuge in such a city are intended by God to encounter his merciful countenance who, Jerome points out quoting Ezekiel, takes no "delight in the death of the wicked" but rather takes "delight when he turns from his wicked ways and lives (Ezekiel 18:23 ISV)."[35] These places of refuge are to be safe zones from those seeking vengeance principally because, as Paul teaches we are "never [to] avenge yourselves, but leave it to the wrath

---

[35] Franke, 88.

of God; for it is written, 'Vengeance is mine, I will repay, says the Lord (Romans 12:19 RSV)." How did God repay for the collective sin of killing his son? – by offering forgiveness, as Benedict XVI points out. When God repays we are to "remember that Jesus' blood speaks a different language from the blood of Abel (Heb 12:24): it does not cry out for vengeance and punishment; it brings reconciliation. It is not poured out against anyone; it is poured out for many, for all. "All have sinned and fall short of the glory of God. . . God put [Jesus] forward as an expiation by his blood" (Rom 3:23, 25)."[36]

[37]

---

[36] Joseph Ratzinger, *Joseph Ratzinger, Benedict XVI, Selected Writings, Faith and Politics*, trans. Michael J. Miller (San Francisco: Ignatius Press, 2018), Kindle Location 546.

[37] Illustrators of Charles Foster, The Story of the Bible, Philadelphia: A.J. Homan Co., 1884. [Public domain], "Fleeing to the City of Refuge (Numbers

Section Questions

1. According to the Church Fathers, how are the Cities of Refuge fulfilled Sacramentally?

35:11-28). From Charles Foster, The Story of the Bible, 1884," https://commons.wikimedia.org/wiki/File:Foster_Story_OTB_173_FleeingToTheCityOfRefuge.jpg.

Judges

[1]

Introduction

As long as Joshua was alive, he was able to prevent his people from

[1] Gustave Doré [Public domain], "Deborah portrayed in Gustave Doré's illustrations for La Grande Bible de Tours (1865)," https://commons.wikimedia.org/wiki/File:053.Deborah_Praises_Jael.jpg.

committing spiritual adultery by idolizing a created reality, or by worshipping false gods. After he dies, the Israelites repeatedly fall into grievous sin. God calls them back to true worship and upright living by inspiring eleven men and one woman, consecutively, to guide their people. When one of these charismatic leaders is no longer needed, he or she fade into the background without creating a dynasty. Hence, they are called judges and not kings. The judges are typically divided into six major judges and six minor judges. The major judges are Othniel, Ehud, Deborah, Gideon, Jephthah, and Samson. The minor judges are Shamgar, Tola, Jair, Ibzan, Elon, and Abdon. These eleven men and one woman that God chooses to guide His people are, points out Hahn, "the kinds of persons whom ancient societies least expected to do great things."[2] For example, explains Hahn, Gideon is at times overwhelmed by fear and feelings of inadequacy all indications of a lack of trust and faith in God who choose him (Judges 6).

In agreement with Hanh, Miller interprets Gideon's objection to God "My clan is the weakest in Manasseh (Judges 6:15 *RSVCE*)" as "meaning that Gideon sees his best hope as having sufficient military power… numbers and strength while God tries to teach him to depend on divine assistance, instead."[3] In eliciting from Gideon greater trust in God and less in human force, God greatly reduces Gideon's army set to battle the Midianites (Judges 7:1-8).

Samson also lacked faith in God and preferred to trust more in his cunning and in his great physical strength. The two judges Shamgar

---

[2] Scott Hahn and Curtis Mitch, *Judges and Ruth* (San Francisco: Ignatius Press, 2015), 14.

[3] Robert D. Miller II, *Understanding the Old Testament* (Chantilly: The Teaching Company, 2019), 171-172.

and Jephthah are surprising picks by God since neither comes from an established, respected family; Similarly, Shamgar, who wielded a farming tool as his main weapon, is the son of a farmer, while Jephthah's mother is a prostitute. Finally, Deborah is surprising since despite being a woman in a society dominated by men God still chooses her, and through her frees the Israelites from Canaanite oppression.[4]

Also included among these accounts of twelve judges is an account of a king, Abimelech one of the sons of the judge Gideon. Despite his people's request to make him a king, the father of Abimelech, Gideon, refused with "I will not rule over you, and my son will not rule over you; the Lord will rule over you. (Judges 8:23 *RSVCE*)." His son, Abimelech, however, gave into the people's request and into his own lust for power by declaring himself as king. By proclaiming himself king, Abimelech tried to replace the temporary leadership of the judges with a monarchy and in his evil zeal murdered his seventy brothers. God "repaid the crime of Abimelech (Judges 9:56 RSV)" by providentially permitting a woman to kill him by dropping a millstone on his head.[5] We will reflect on the spiritual lessons this one king and twelve judges have to offer by beginning with the Judges as a whole, and then by focusing on a few prominent judges.

Section Questions

1. Distinguish the Judges from the Kings. Include the following

---

[4] Hahn and Curtis Mitch, 14.

[5] John Bergsma and Brant Pitre, *A Catholic Introduction to the Bible, Volume I* (San Francisco: Ignatius Press, 2018), 320.

in your answer: Dynasties, Charismatic.

Judges as a Whole

Abimelech's brief evil reign reflects the tenor of the entire book of Judges as the last verse of the book indicates, "In those days there was no king in Israel; every man did what was right in his own eyes (Judges 21:25 *RSVCE*)." This verse does not necessarily mean that the solution to the moral depravity was a human king since prior to the book of Judges the Israelites did not have a human king and instead saw God as their king who raised up prophetic and charismatic leaders when needed to direct them (1 Samuel 12:12).

In the case of the book of Judges, God inspires Judges to lead His people according to a noticeable, states Pitre, "spiritual pattern" described in chapter two.[6] The pattern entails three stages that cyclically repeat. First, the Israelites do "evil in the sight of the Lord (Judges 2:11 *RSVCE*) and begin to worship the false gods of their neighbors. Second, the Israelites are conquered by their enemies and cruelly ruled by them. This leads the Israelites to cry out to God for help who answers their cry by raising "up judges, who saved them out of the power of those who plundered them (Judges 2:16 *RSVCE*)." Eventually, though, the cycle begins again during a time of relative peace and prosperity when the Israelites stop obeying the judge sent to them (Judges 2:17), and begin to excessively desire money, power, and pleasure accompanied by worship of false Gods.

This pattern is evident in our lives, comments Pitre, "What the

---

[6] Brant Pitre, *The Old Testament-A Historical and Theological Journey through Jewish Scripture,* MP 16.

Bible is teaching us here is that temporal surplus and temporal blessing can be a very dangerous thing spiritually also. It is very easy to forget the Lord when everything looks good and everything looks well. Sometimes it is precisely in slavery and servitude and being caught in sin that people actually open up to God."[7] It is important to add that the referred to surplus and blessing may not necessarily have been obtained by evil means.

Pitre explains that, a period of time when the faith is severely tested and in which countless sacrifices are made may be followed by an experience of growth and plenty. This time of success, however, bears within it a temptation to be lazy, forget to pray, forget that God is central and the risk of falling gradually into idolatry where the goods of this world take precedence over God even when appearances may indicate otherwise, such as growth of Catholic schools, church attendance, vocations etc.[8] Growth, success, even when Catholic, can tempt a person to be proud and haughty by which one looks down upon others and forgets, or ignores, that the success and growth are primarily gifts from God to be humbly shared with others. The book of Proverbs warns, "Pride goes before destruction, a haughty spirit before a fall (Proverbs 16:18 *RSVCE*)." The reason the Israelites were frequently tested and "constantly oppressed by the onslaught of the nations," asserts John Cassian, was precisely as a way that God used to heal the Israelite's haughty spirit:

---

[7] Pitre, MP 16.

[8] Pitre, MP 16. Bergsma and Pitre cite Judges 18 on Micah and Dan as an example of pride expressed by liturgical abuse, and an example among many where the book of Judges presents "counterexample[s]: how things ought not to be done." Bergsma and Pitre, 327.

> Thus, constantly oppressed by the onslaught of the nations, they would never feel that they did not need the Lord's help. Hence, they would always meditate on him and cry out to him, and they would neither lapse into sluggish inactivity nor lose their ability to fight and their training in virtue. For frequently security and prosperity have brought low those whom adversities cannot overcome.[9]

Interestingly, as described in Judges, Israel grew spiritually during times of persecution and declined by falling into sin during times of relative peace and harmony with other nations. As Bergsma and Pitre observe:

> it is a sobering moral insight that, according to the book of Judges, it was precisely during the times of peace and "rest"—economic, military, and national prosperity won by the judges—that the people of Israel were most inclined to forget about God and fall back into sin. After that, 'whenever the judge died, they turned back and behaved worse than their fathers' (Judg 2:19). Judges makes clear that each generation must learn afresh the lesson of its dependence on God.[10]

An example of this pattern of reform, prosperity and pride, and downfall and humiliations is a person who amends his life,

---

[9] John R. Franke, *Ancient Christian Commentary on Scripture: Old Testament IV, Joshua, Judges, Ruth, 1-2 Samuel* (Downers Grove: Intervarsity Press, 2014), 109.

[10] Bergsma and Pitre, 335.

successfully brings many to repentance and conversion and then falls into temptation by excessively delighting in the success, fame, influence, honors received and money acquired. As the centrality of God in his life is displaced the person begins to pridefully seek earthly goods for self-glorification. If this person is religious and/or a cleric he might also express pride by liturgical abuse, either directly by disregarding norms for flimsy reasons or may, on the other hand, follow laws scrupulously but in an ostentatious manner and even angry manner where he presents himself as a domineering prince of the act of worship.[11]

According to Isaac of Nineveh the reason God allowed the pagan nations to be in constant tension with Israel and at times to even defeat the Israelites was to help ensure the Israelites remained humble. When the Israelites experienced humiliating defeats, they became more aware of their limitations and weaknesses, which in turn served as an opportunity to rely more on God in gratitude for all the gifts bestowed upon them. In applying this lesson to the individual, Isaac of Nineveh writes:

> For the righteous man who has no consciousness of his own weakness walks on a razor's edge, and is never far from falling, nor from the ravening lion— I mean the demon of pride. And again, a man who does not know his own weakness falls short of humility; and he who falls short of this, also falls short of

[11] Pitre, MP 16. Bergsma and Pitre cite Judges 18 on Micah and Dan as an example of pride expressed by liturgical abuse, and an example among many where the book of Judges presents "counterexample[s]: how things ought not to be done." Bergsma and Pitre, 327.

> perfection; and he who falls short of perfection is forever held by dread, because his city is not founded on pillars of iron, neither upon lintels of brass, that is, humility.[12]

Jesus' Parable of the Pharisee and the Tax Collector similarly teaches that times of downfall, dishonor, failure and obvious sin often coincide with times of cooperation with grace, humility and conversion. In contrast, times of success, outward manifestations virtue, and public recognition of being successful and virtuous often coincide with growth in pride and a consequent resistance to continual conversion. In explaining this paradox Benedict XVI writes,

> If the tax collector with all his undisputed sins stands more justified before God than the Pharisee with all his undeniably good works (Lk 18:9-14), this is not because the sins of the tax collector were not sins or because the good deeds of the Pharisee were not good deeds. Nor does it mean that the good that man does is not good before God, or the evil, not evil or at least not particularly important. The reason for this paradoxical judgment of God is shown precisely from our question. The Pharisee no longer knows that he, too, has guilt. He has a completely clear conscience. But this silence of conscience makes him impenetrable to God and men, while the cry of conscience that plagues the tax collector makes him capable of truth and love. Jesus can move sinners. Not hiding behind the screen of their erroneous consciences, they have not become unreachable for the change that God expects of

---

[12] Franke, 108.

> them—of us. He is ineffective with the "righteous" because they are not aware of any need for forgiveness and conversion. Their consciences no longer accuse them but justify them.[13]

Often God will respond to proud people who are closed in on themselves, teaches Aquinas, by providentially permitting the proud person, who may even take pride in his conversion, to fall into sexual sin so that by a more obvious sin the person may repent of his worst and more hidden sin of pride:

> by allowing them to fall into sins of the flesh, which though they be less grievous are more evidently shameful. ... From this indeed the gravity of pride is made manifest. For just as a wise physician, in order to cure a worse disease, allows the patient to contract one that is less dangerous, so the sin of pride is shown to be more grievous by the very fact that, as a remedy, God allows men to fall into other sins.[14]

Repeatedly in the time of the Judges the Israelites forget God as central, forget that God is Father of all "Israel is my first-born son (Exodus 4:22 *RSVCE*),"[15] who desires all to live together in a shared

---

[13] Joseph Ratzinger, *Faith and Politics, Selected Writings*, trans. Michael J. Miller and others (San Francisco: Ignatius Press, 2018), kindle locations 1231-1241.

[14] Thomas Aquinas, "Summa Theologica," II-II, Q. 162, Art. 6, Ad. 3, newadvent.org, http://www.newadvent.org/summa/3162.htm .

[15] Marianne Meye Thompson, *Promise of the Father: Jesus and God in the New Testament* (Louisville: Westminster John Knox Press, 2000), 35-56.

freedom as His adopted children by which at minimum the Ten Commandments are followed. These Ten Commandments, reflective of natural law, provide the basic framework of living in accordance with our social nature. This participated freedom, safeguarded by following the Ten Commandments, Benedict XVI describes as a freedom in which we coexist harmoniously with others.[16]

Judges portrays many variations on the theme of individualistic freedom defined by each person choosing in an unrestrained manner what to do without concern of others. During this time of rampant individualism and relativism, instead of God being recognized as a Father who has instilled in our nature a moral code to follow so that we can all participate in freedom and benefit from mutual support, many choose instead do act as kings in competition with other kings. As kings in savage competition with one another, the moral law universally written on the hearts of all is ignored and out of lust for power and the desire to dominate horrific deeds are committed including, fratricide (Judges 9), child sacrifice (Judges 11), treating women as objects, rape, dismemberment (Judges 19), and civil war (Judges 20), in which the tribe of Benjamin is almost completely wiped out of existence.

These terrible occurrences serve as reminders of what a society can eventually become and do when the centrality of God as Father and the commandments the Heavenly Father has instilled in our social

---

Among many passages that explicitly and implicitly identify God as Father, Thompson cites: Exodus 4:22-23; Deuteronomy 32:4-18; Hosea 11:1; Isaiah 63:16, 64:8-9.

[16] Benedict XVI, *Day by Day with Pope Benedict XVI*, ed. Peter John Cameron (San Francisco: Ignatius Press, 2006), 96.

nature are ignored and instead people vie to replace God as kings as they live according to a relativistic, ever changing moral code defined principally by immediate self-interest. The Book of Judges' concentration of sinful, evil actions by the Israelites serves a particular role in Sacred Scripture that not only depicts human behavior in union with God at its best but also human nature divorced from divine grace at its worst. In the words of Bergsma and Pitre, "Judges is largely a counterexample: how things ought not to be done."[17]

[18]

One particularly gruesome account involves a Levite, an Israelite from the priestly tribe, arriving in the Benjamite city of Gibeah and

[17] Bergsma and Pitre, 327.

[18] James Tissot [Public domain], "The_Levite_finds_his_concubine_lying_on_the_doorstep,_James_Tissot.jpg (541 × 355 pixels, file size: 47 KB, MIME type: image/jpeg)," https://commons.wikimedia.org/wiki/File:The_Levite_finds_his_concubine_lying_on_the_doorstep,_James_Tissot.jpg.

being inhospitably received. Eventually he is welcomed by an old man who gives the Levite and the Levite's concubine shelter. While inside a crowd of unruly men gather outside. These men demand the male guest come out so that they can "know him," euphemistic language for sexual relations. Instead, the old man offers his daughter and the Levite's concubine to these lecherous men. The Levite responds by "seizing his concubine" and forcing her outside where she is repeatedly raped by the men. At dawn, the Levite open the doors, sees that she is almost dead, and rudely order her "Get up, let us be going (Judges 19:28 *RSVCE*)." When she does not respond he lays her on his donkey and leaven. Upon arriving home, he cut her into twelve pieces and send her dismembered body to representatives of the various tribes. When word gets out of what occurred, eleven tribes band together, attack the tribe of Benjamin and, in so doing, almost completely kill all the tribe of Benjamin.

Pitre compares the Levite's uncaring manner of relating to his concubine with Adam's failure to obey God's order to guard/keep *shamar* (Genesis 2:15 שָׁמַר) the garden and its inhabitants in particular the woman Eve who would soon be created as a suitable companion and friend of Adam.[19] Both Adam and the Levite fail to be priestly guardians of the holy, in particular women, created, along with Adam, in the image and likeness of God. In a way both serve as, states Pitre, "anti-Christ[s]" who refuse to lay down their lives for their brides, an action that Jesus Christ will do with his death on the cross. [20]

---

[19] Pitre, MP 17.

[20] Pitre, MP 17.

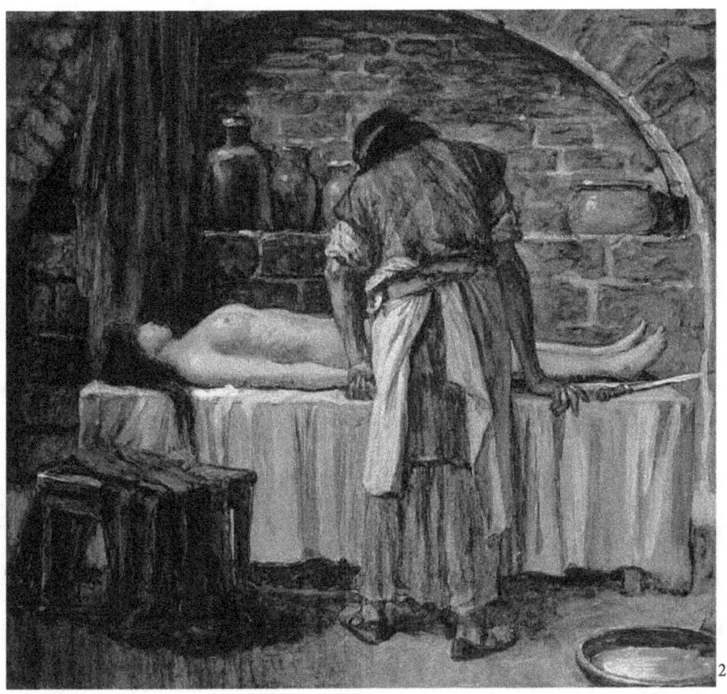
[21]

Section Questions

1. Choose one of the following Judges and explain how this judge specifically was chosen by God as one whom people least thought would be chosen as a leader: Gideon, Shamgar, Jephthah, Deborah

2. Compare Adam and the Levite in Judges 19:28 with Jesus. With specific reference to Scripture, include the following in your answer: Guardian, Bride, Counterexample

---

[21] James Tissot [Public domain], "The Levite Before The Corpse Of His Wife, James Tissot," https://commons.wikimedia.org/wiki/File:The_Levite_Before_The_Corpse_Of_His_Wife_by_James_Tissot.jpg.

Jephthah

Jephthah is an example of a judge who although acting as a guardian of his people on behalf of God does so in a way that undermines his role as God's delegate. He treats the false God Chemosh, who Jephthah mistakenly identifies as a God of the Ammonites as, writes Miller, "a legitimate god, doing things for his people, just as Yahweh does things for the Israelite people (Judges 11:24)."[22] By approaching the true God in this distorted manner, Jephthah presents, continues Miller, "a false version of the true faith: the wrong worship of the right God."[23] Another way that Jephthah undermines his role as delegate includes the horrific killing of many, including forty-two thousand Israelites of the tribe of Ephraim (Judges 12:6). Prior to this intertribal slaughter, Jephthah angrily accused the Ephraimites, "I and my people had a great feud with the Ammonites; and when I called you, you did not deliver me from their hand (Judges 12:2 *RSVCE*)."

Before fighting with his brother tribe, the Ephraimites, Jephthah fought the Ammonites, the enemy of Israel collectively understood. Jephthah did so by first promising that if he is successful in battle then he will sacrifice to God the first person as whom he meets upon returning home as "a burnt offering (Judges 11:31 *RSVCE*)." "With this vow," comments Miller, Jephthah "tries to serve Yahweh the way one would serve those other gods … [as] a Moabite king offers his own

---

[22] Robert D. Miller II, *Understanding the Old Testament* (Chantilly: The Teaching Company, 2019), 175.

[23] Miller, 177.

child to Chemosh—the very god Jephthah equates with Yahweh."[24] The first person who greeted him was his daughter along with other women who came out to greet him "with timbrels and with dances (Judges 11:34 *RSVCE*)." This is not surprising since, explains Irene Nowell, women typically honored victorious warriors with a dance. An early example that Nowell cites is Moses' sister Miriam who celebrated the Israelite defeat of the Egyptians by leading all the women "with timbrels and dancing (Exodus 15:20 *RSVCE*)."

[25]

Some scholars think it is possible that Jephthah's daughter may

---

[24] Miller, 177.

[25] Alexandre Cabanel [Public domain], "The Daughter of Jephthah, by Alexandre Cabanel (1879)," https://commons.wikimedia.org/wiki/File: Alexandre_Cabanel_-_The_Daughter_of_Jephthah_(1879,_Oil_on_canvas).JPG.

have not been literally offered to God in flames since it is possible to interpret the passage as implying that the sacrifice of virginity is of similar value to a burnt offering. In addition, these scholars add that Judges only describes his daughter as mourning being a virgin and not for being condemned to death. However, it is also reasonable to hold that she mourns her virginity because she will be offered up as a burnt offering with no prospect of marrying before being burned.[26]

Ambrose compares Jephthah's commitment to keep his vow to sacrifice the first person who greets him even if this person is his daughter with King Herod's commitment to give Herodias anything she wanted "even half of my kingdom (Mark 6:23 *RSVCE*)." When Herodias asks for John the Baptist's head, like Jephthah Herod does not break his oath but orders the beheading of John and the head given to Herodias. According to Ambrose, "It is also sometimes contrary to duty to fulfill a promise or to keep an oath. As was the case with Herod, who swore that whatever was asked he would give to the daughter of Herodias, and so allowed the death of John, that he might not break his word. And what shall I say of Jephthah, who offered up his daughter in sacrifice..."[27]

Although Jephthah and King Herod both represent distorted ways of keeps one's words by following through on promises, their example should not lessen the importance of being true to one's words by fulfilling one's promises. Provided that the promises made are essentially good, the intention is properly ordered to God and the circumstances are appropriate keeping one's word, making good one's

---

[26] Bergsma and Pitre, 326. Bergsma and Pitre refer to 1 Samuel 2:22; Exodus 13:1, 11-16; Judges 11:37-40.

[27] Franke, 138-139.

promises is an essential teaching early on the Old Testament as is evident in Moses' words to the Israelites, "This is what the Lord has commanded. When a man vows a vow to the Lord or swears an oath to bind himself by a pledge, he shall not break his word; he shall do all according to all the proceeds out of his mouth (Numbers 30:1-2 *RSVCE*)." Similarly, Deuteronomy teaches, "You shall be careful to perform what has passed your lips, for you have voluntarily vowed to the Lord your God what you have promised with your mouth (Deuteronomy 23:23 *RSVCE*)."

Echoing this teaching on our obligation to be like God who is true to his word, the incarnate Word of God, Jesus Christ taught, "Let what you say be simply 'Yes' or 'No' (Matthew 5:37 *RSVCE*)." This principle applies whether or not one has made a formal oath or not for God is true to his Word at all times. Since God fulfills what He says we also ought "to be doers of the word (James 1:22 *RSVCE*)."

Section Questions

1. Compare Jephthah with King Herod. With specific reference to Scripture, include the following in your answer: Jephthah's Daughter, John the Baptist, Vow, Pride.

Deborah

Amidst the deplorable treatment of women in Judges is a heroine and judge, Deborah. Deborah lived during a time when the Israelites were suffering under the harsh rule of the Canaanites. God inspired Deborah to tell Barak to lead an army against the Canaanite army. Barak does and he successfully defeats the Canaanite army in battle.

Sisera, the commander of the Canaanite army, flees from the battle and takes us shelter in the tent of a woman, Jael. Jael offers him milk and when Sisera is asleep, she quickly kills him by hammering a tent peg into his skull.

[28]

For Ambrose, the two women Deborah and Jael foreshadow the Church which likewise as a strong woman leads her children to successfully defeat.[29] When referring to the Church, Ambrose is at the same time referring to Mary who perfectly embodies the Church, for Mary, writes Ambrose "is the type of the Church, which is also married

---

[28] James Tissot [Public domain], "Jael Shows to Barak, Sisera Lying Dead, c. 1896-1902, by James Jacques Joseph Tissot (French, 1836-1902) or followers, gouache on board, 5 1/2 x 9 7/16 in. (14 x 24 cm), at the Jewish Museum, New York," https://commons.wikimedia.org/wiki/File:Tissot_Jael_Shows_to_Barak,_Sisera_Lying_Dead.jpg

[29] Franke, 116.

but remains immaculate."[30] At the end of time, as first prophesied in Genesis chapter three, Mary and her seed (Christ and his mystical body the Church), will crush the head of Satan (Genesis 3:15; Revelation 12). The crushing of the skull of an evil military commander by the woman Jael is a sign of this future more important victory when the spiritual power behind evil world rulers, such as Sisera, will be definitively defeated.

In referring to the spiritual powers that lie behind the wicked St. Paul writes, "For we are not contending against flesh and blood, but against the principalities, against the powers, against the world rulers of this present darkness, against the spiritual hosts of wickedness in the heavenly places (Ephesians 6:12 *RSVCE*)."[31] With these words, Paul is teaching what already is found in the Old Testament, an unseen angelic world, the unseen world of created intelligences intertwined with our visible world. As pointed out by Pitre, the prophet Ezekiel states that the actual power behind a very wicked ruler, the King of Tyre was "in Eden the garden of God … [who was] blameless … till iniquity was found in you…[who] was filled with violence, and…sinned." (Ezekiel 28:13-16 *RSVCE*) Here, Ezekiel is identifying the actual power behind this ruler with the angelic tempter from the beginning of time.[32]

---

[30] Luigi Gambero, *Mary and the Fathers of the Church: The Blessed Virgin Mary in Patristic Thought*, trans. Thomas Buffer (San Francisco: Ignatius Press, 1991), 198. Gambero cites the following, *Expositio in Lucam* 2, 7; PL 15, 1635-36.

[31] Pitre, MP3, 7.

[32] Pitre, MP3, 7.

[33]

In accordance with Church wisdom, formed by Biblical wisdom, we should take great caution in claiming that anyone we know is influenced by evil spiritual powers, but, at the same time, we ought to be aware that it is possible, and does occur, and all are vulnerable to these intellectual powers that interface with our world in good and in evil ways.

Section Questions

1. How does Deborah and Jael foreshadow Mary? With specific reference to Scripture, include the following in your answer: Humility, Fall of the Proud, Sisera

[33] James Tissot [Public domain], "Jael Smote Sisera, and Slew Him, circa 1896-1902, by James Jacques Joseph Tissot (French, 1836-1902) or follower, gouache on board, 5 7/16 x 7 3/8 in. (13.9 x 18.8 cm), at the Jewish Museum, New York," https://commons.wikimedia.org/wiki/File:Tissot_Jael_Smote_Sisera,_and_Slew_Him.jpg.

Samson

Like Deborah, Samson defeated Israel's enemies. Unlike Deborah, however, Samson is not known for his virtue but rather for repeatedly misusing his gift of strength until finally God takes away Samson's strength. Samson's name and the name of the woman who deceived him, observes Hahn, represent Samson's gift of strength and loss of this gift. In Hebrew, Samson's name is *Shimshon* (שִׁמְשׁוֹן), which is based on the Hebrew word for sun, *shemesh* (שֶׁמֶשׁ). In contrast, the name of the woman who tricks Samson into breaking his Nazarite vow is Delilah (דְלִילָה). Delilah is related to the Hebrew word for night, *lilah* (לַיְלָה). As night, Delilah, she blocks Samson's strength from shining forth.[34] Ambrose observes that before seducing Samson, Delilah was herself seduced, seduced by love of money promised to her if she could find out Samson's secret to his strength.[35]

The Nazarite vows that Samson breaks, partly by Delilah's deception, are three-fold: no association with dead bodies, no drinking of strong drinks, and no cutting of his hair (Numbers 6:1-21). Samson breaks the first vow by eating honey from a dead lion's body (Judges 14:5-9). He breaks the second by at least placing himself in a near occasion of sin where strong drinks, including alcohol, are typically served in a feast he hosts (Judges 14:10-20). Finally, he breaks the last one by giving way to Delilah who cuts his hair (Judges 16:13-22). According to Bergsma and Pitre, Samson did not lose his gift of strength merely because he allowed his hair to be cut. Rather, he lost his gift after he had broken all three of the Nazarite vows, and by so

---

[34] Hahn and Mitch, loc. 2728.

[35] Franke, 160.

doing severed his relationship with God.[36]

37

After Samson's hair grows back God restores his strength, thereby enabling Samson to bring down a house full of Philistines. As Scripture states, "So the dead whom he slew at his death were more than those whom he had slain during his life (Judges 16:30 *RSVCE*)." A spiritual teaching of this act, comments William A. Anderson, is that God still fulfills his salvific plans even through those who "misuse the gifts that they receive."[38] Despite his many flaws, Samson as judge represented to his people God's will on earth. Our response to imperfect, God

[36] Bergsma and Pitre, 327.

[37] Peter Paul Rubens [Public domain], "Samson Slaying the Lion (1628) by Peter Paul Rubens," https://commons.wikimedia.org/wiki/File:Sans%C3%B3n_matando_al_le%C3%B3n_-_Pedro_Pablo_Rubens.jpg.

[38] William A. Anderson, Liguori Catholic Bible Study, Historical Books I: Joshua, Judges, Ruth, 1 and 2 Samuel (Liguori Catholic Bible Study (Liguori: Liguori Publications, 2013).

given authority figures[39], teaches St. Maximillian Mary Kolbe:

> is obedience and obedience alone that is the sure sign to us of the divine will. A superior may, it is true, make a mistake; but it is impossible for us to be mistaken in obeying a superior's command. The only exception to this rule is the case of a superior commanding something that in even the slightest way would contravene God's law. Such a superior would not be conveying God's will.[40]

41

---

[39] (Romans 13:1-2 *RSVCE*) "Let every person be subject to the governing authorities. For there is no authority except from God, and those that exist have been instituted by God."

[40] "From a letter of Maximillian Mary Kolbe (Scritti del P. Massimiliano M. Kolbe, Italian translation, vol. I, pt, 1 [Padua, 1971], 75-77,166)," liturgies.net, http://www.liturgies.net/saints/maximiliankolbe/readings.htm.

[41] Gustave Doré [Public domain], "According to the biblical narrative, Samson died when he grasped two pillars of the Temple of Dagon and

The essential reason why we are to obey authority figures, unless they command us, or try to persuade us, to sin is found in the life of Christ who "humbled himself and became obedient unto death, even death on a cross (Philippians 2:8 *RSVCE*)." By this obedience and subsequent Resurrection, Christ renewed a disobedient world in which relationships are typically marked by violence and death. As Benedict XVI writes:

> The One who is truly like God does not hold graspingly to his autonomy, to the limitlessness of his ability and his willing. He does the contrary: he becomes completely dependent; he becomes a slave. Because he does not go the route of power but that of love, he can descend into the depths of Adam's lie, into the depths of death, and there raise up truth and life. Thus, Christ is the new Adam, with whom humankind begins anew. The Son, who is by nature relationship and relatedness, reestablishes relationships. His arms, spread out on the cross, are an open invitation to relationship, which is continually offered to us. The cross, the place of his obedience, is the true tree of life.[42]

Due to Samson's many imperfections and many sins it can be

'bowed himself with all his might' (Judges 16:30, KJV). This has been variously interpreted as Samson pushing the pillars apart (left) or pulling them together (right)," https://commons.wikimedia.org/wiki/File:064.The_Death_of_Samson.jpg.

[42] Benedict XVI, *Day by Day with Pope Benedict XVI*, ed. Peter John Cameron (San Francisco: Ignatius Press, 2006), 56.

difficult to recognize him as one appointed by God to be obeyed, but what can be even more difficult is to see Samson as a type of Christ. Church Fathers, though, see this typology, especially in Samson's and Christ's deaths. At the moment of their deaths both were victorious over their enemies, Samson physically and Christ spiritually. As Caesarius of Arles writes:

> Therefore, his enemies brought him to play the buffoon before them." Notice here an image of the cross. Samson extends his hands spread out to the two columns as to the two beams of the cross. Moreover, by his death he overcame his adversaries, because his sufferings became the death of his persecutors. For this reason, Scripture concludes as follows: "Those he killed at his death were more than those he had killed during his lifetime." This mystery was clearly fulfilled in our Lord Jesus Christ, for at his death he completed our redemption which he had by no means publicly announced during his life: who lives and reigns forever and ever.[43]

Section Questions

1. According to Caesarius of Arles, how does Samson specifically foreshadow Jesus?

2. With respect to the meaning of Samson's name in Hebrew and the meaning of Delilah's name in Hebrew, how does Delilah prevent Samson from fulfilling his mission as a judge?

---

[43] Franke, 167.

Ruth

[1]

Introduction

The Book of Ruth contrasts with the preceding Book of Judges. Unlike the Book of Judges which, with some exceptions, provides multiple descriptions of leaders and people acting immorally, the Book of Ruth, states Bergsma and Pitre, provide an account of Israelites and one non-Israelite acting in an exemplary manner.[2] While the positive

---

[1] William Blake [Public domain], "Naomi entreating Ruth and Orpah to return to the land of Moab by William Blake, 1795," https://commons.wikimedia.org/wiki/File:1795-William-Blake-Naomi-entreating-Ruth-Orpah.jpg.

[2] John Bergsma and Brant Pitre, *A Catholic Introduction to the Bible, Volume I* (San Francisco: Ignatius Press, 2018), 334.

moral lesson of the Book of Ruth is virtually indisputable, scholars disagree on its literary classification. Some maintain that it is historical, other argue that it is fictional, a novella etc. Likewise, it is debated when it was authored. Some hold it was written as early as the tenth century B.C., while others posit that it was written as late at the fifth century B.C.[3]

Contributing to this debate, Hahn argues that:

> [T]here are several reasons for considering the Book of Ruth a historical short story. Besides the fact that it portrays accurately the conditions of life in a rural community in biblical times, the story is situated in a known historical period (time of the judges, 1:1), unfolds in known historical places (Moab, Bethlehem), and makes reference to known historical persons (Jesse, David). Its historiographical intent is also suggested by the concluding genealogy, which anchors the account in Israel's sacred history. Indeed, the same pre-Davidic bloodline that appears in 4:18-22 is presented elsewhere in the Bible as authentic archival information (1 Chron 2:5-15). Finally, it is highly improbable that a writer of fiction would make David's great-grandmother Ruth a Moabite rather than a faithful Israelite, especially since David himself conquered the Moabites and made them vassals subject to Israel (2 Sam 8:2).[4]

---

[3] Scott Hahn and Curtis Mitch, *Judges and Ruth* (San Francisco: Ignatius Press, 2015), 57.

[4] Hahn and Mitch, 58.

As Hahn points out, the first verse of the Book of Ruth situate the entire narrative within a particular historical time, near the end of the time of the Judges and before the establishment of monarchy, "In the days when the judges ruled there was a famine in the land, and a certain man of Bethlehem in Judah went to sojourn in the country of Moab… (Ruth 1:1 *RSVCE*)" This verse indicates that the setting is, states Hahn, "around 1100 B.C."[5]

[6]

Subsequent verses identify the Bethlehemite man as Elimelech. He is accompanied by his wife, Naomi, and two sons. They settle in Moab. Sadly, while in Moab, Elimelech dies, leaving behind his wife and two sons, who had by this married. The two sons in turn also die, leaving

---

[5] Hahn and Mitch, 66.

[6] Francesco Hayez [Public domain], "Portrait of a woman as Ruth (c. 1853) by Francesco Hayez," https://commons.wikimedia.org/wiki/File:Hayez_A_woman_as_Ruth.jpg.

behind three widows, their mother Naomi, and their two wives, Orpah and Ruth. Naomi decides to return to Bethlehem. Ruth insists on accompanying her while Orpah remains in Moab. In Bethlehem, Naomi introduces Ruth to Boaz, related to her husband Elimelech. Eventually, Boaz agrees to marry Ruth, and Ruth becomes a member of the genealogy of the Israelite people, including being part of King David's and Jesus' lineage.

We will reflect on this outlined narrative in relationship to providence, women, and typology.

Section Questions

1. According to Bergsma and Pitre how does the book of Ruth contrast with the book of Judges? Include the following in your response: Fidelity, Ruth, Naomi, Judges

Providence

Although God's providential shaping of history in the Book of Ruth is not spectacular as it is, at times in Exodus, nonetheless, points out Hahn, "there is a sense that even the most ordinary events are guided by his hidden hand. At several critical steps, readers witness divine 'coincidences' in which the Lord steers the actions of this family and blesses them…"[7] God's guiding of ordinary events, Hahn explains, is stated right in chapter one when Naomi decides to return to Israel upon learning that "the Lord had visited his people and given them food (Ruth 1:6 *RSVCE*)."

---

[7] Hahn and Mitch, 58.

Bergsma and Pitre, observe that the text which comes before this explicit verse of God's providence, God's providential guidance is implied in the name of Naomi's father and in the name of Bethlehem. In Hebrew, Elimelech (אֱלִימֶלֶךְ) means "God is king" while Bethlehem means (בֵּית לֶחֶם) "House of Bread".[8] As the ultimate king, God guided and protected Elimelech and his family, including during times when they lacked bread. However, as in many cases in history, how God did this is not immediately clear, especially when considering that due to a famine Elimelech left Bethlehem and traveled to the land of the Moabites, a people who were held in suspicion by the Israelites because, according the Genesis, they were the offspring of an incestuous relationship between Lot and one of his daughters (Genesis 19:35-37), and for the reason that the Moabites had once conquered and oppressed the Israelites before the judge Ehud delivered them (Judges 3:12-30). Interestingly, the very name Moab (מוֹאָב) literally means from father, ab (אָב), father, and mo (מוֹ), from, since the child of Lot's daughter gave birth to her father's child.

The Church Fathers identified the providence in these seemingly disordered events by recognizing God, governing "sweetly (Wisdom 8:1 *DRA*)" behind the scenes, preparing for the coming of his Son who would gather all people into the Catholic Church. Elimelech's traveling to the Moabites led to the Moabite woman Ruth returning back to Israel with Elimelech's wife Naomi. In Bethlehem, Ruth was incorporated into the genealogy of Israel, the genealogy of King David, and of Jesus Christ, of the house of David, "Boaz the father of Obed by

---

[8] "458. Elimelek," biblehub.com, https://biblehub.com/hebrew/458.htm. "1035. Beth Lechem," biblehub.com, https://biblehub.com/hebrew/1035.htm.

Ruth, and Obed the father of Jesse, and Jesse the father of David the king…and Jacob the father of Joseph the husband of Mary of whom Jesus was born (Matthew 1:5-16 *RSVCE*)."

As Ambrose states, the Moabite Ruth "prefigures all of us who were gathered from the nations for the purpose of joining the church of the Lord."[9] John Chrysostom, points out that Ruth was not accepted into Israel, which prefigures the Church as a New Israel, until after Ruth had left "her parents and her nation and her native land" in a similar way as the Catholic Church is "not made loveable to her spouse [Christ] before she had forsaken her prior customs." Chrysostom then quotes from Psalm 45, "Hear, O daughter, consider, and incline you ear; forget your people and your father's house (Psalm 45:10 *RSVCE*)."[10]

We who are members of the Church are likewise to detach ourselves of any customs of this world including those we have been taught by our nationality if they are opposed to the ways of God as revealed in Jesus Christ, as St. Paul exhorts, "Put off the old man that belongs to your former manner of life and is corrupt through deceitful lusts, and be renewed in the spirit of your minds, and put on the new man, created after the likeness of God in true righteousness and holiness (Ephesians 4:22-24 *RSVCE*)." Jesus likewise promises, "everyone who has left houses or brothers or sisters or father or mother or children or lands, for my name's sake, will receive a hundredfold, and inherit eternal life (Matthew 19: 29 *RSVCE*)." Ruth

---

[9] John R. Franke, *Ancient Christian Commentary on Scripture: Old Testament IV, Joshua, Judges, Ruth, 1-2 Samuel* (Downers Grove: Intervarsity Press, 2014), 181.

[10] Franke, 191.

who sacrificed her lands and her people for the sake of her mother-in-law, a poor widow, would be later rewarded, observes St. Jerome, by being made "an ancestress of Christ."[11] Without realizing it, by caring for the least of society in the eyes of the world, a poor widow, Naomi served Christ for as He teaches "as you did it to one of the least of my brethren, you did it to me (Matthew 25:40 *RSVCE*)." Christ, in turn, rewarded her by including Ruth in his genealogy.

[12]

[11] Bergsma and Pitre, 350.

[12] Julius Schnorr von Carolsfeld [Public domain], "Julius Schnorr von Carolsfeld: Ruth in Boaz's Field, 1828," https://commons.wikimedia.org/wiki/File:Julius_Schnorr_von_Carolsfeld-_Ruth_im_Feld_des_Boaz.jpg.

Section Questions

1. How specifically does Chrysostom and Jerome spiritually interpret Ruth's decision to leave behind her people? Include the following in your response: Love, Promised Land, Rewarded

Women

As classified by the Pentateuch, Naomi, and her mother-in-law represent two classes of vulnerable people: the immigrant, and the widow. The third class of vulnerable people are orphans (Exodus 22:21-22; Deuteronomy 24:19). The Israelites were commanded by God to treat these people with respect and provide for their needs. For example, Deuteronomy commands the Israelites not to go back over their vineyard after the grapes have been picked so that the overlooked grapes can be picked by those in need (Deuteronomy 24:21).

Heeding this command, Boaz allows Ruth to glean his fields after they have been picked. He also protects her by ordering his young male workers not to molest Ruth and goes further by even telling them to help her by pulling "out some from the bundles for her (Ruth 2:16 *RSVCE*)." Bergsma and Pitre contrast Boaz's uprightness with the proceeding Book of Judges' mistreatment of the vulnerable, especially of women, including kidnapping, sexual and physical abuse, human sacrifice, murder, and dismemberment. They explain that "the canonical juxtaposition of the book of Ruth with the book of Judges makes clear that the treatment of women in Judges was non-normative and contrary to the spirit of the covenant; in Ruth the sacred author clearly provides a model or "*prescriptive*" narrative for the relationship between the sexes."[13]

Boaz demonstrates his exemplary virtue even further by restraining himself when Ruth offers herself to him with the words "spread your garment over your maidservant." These words are understood as provocative when the context is remembered. Ruth said these words after she slipped onto the threshing floor where Boaz had gone to sleep for the night. There she uncovered Boaz's feet, which often, comments Miller, are an implied reference to a man's private parts.[14] After uncovering Boaz's "feet," or intimate parts, Ruth lays down close by him. At midnight Boaz awoke and "was startled (Ruth 3:8 *RSVCE*)" by seeing her laying at his "feet". She asked him to spread his garment over her. Restraining himself he told her that first he must allow a closer relative who also may be interested in marrying her the opportunity to propose to her. Boaz then ensured that Ruth left early in the morning, unseen by anyone, so that her honor would be kept.[15]

In praising Boaz's chastity, Theodoret of Cyr writes, "The man was so virtuous that he did not rush into a marriage outside the law, but he spoke with his neighbors about the marriage. ... Furthermore, because he was not serving lust, he took her in the spirit that one should take a wife."[16] In the patristic era work *Opus Imperfectum in Matthaeum*, attributed to John Chrysostom, Boaz is described as not daring to touch her "as a lascivious man would," nor being overwhelmed by her

---

[13] Bergsma and Pitre, 343.

[14] Robert D. Miller II, *Understanding the Old Testament* (Chantilly: The Teaching Company, 2019), 231.

[15] Bergsma and Pitre, 344.

[16] Franke, 191. *Questions on Ruth* is cited, "MEIT (Ruth), 35; PG 80: 525, no. 351-52".

youthful beauty as a "mature man might be of a young woman" nor excessively fearing, abhorring her as some chaste men would. Instead, Boaz, in anticipation of Christ's perfect chastity, treated Ruth with restraint, respect and dignity.[17]

[18]

[17] Franke, 188. Homily 1, of the *Incomplete Work on Matthew* is cited, "MEIT (Ruth), 34; PG 56: 619".

[18] William de Brailes [Public domain], "Top - Ruth Meets Boaz as she gleans," https://commons.wikimedia.org/wiki/File:William_de_Brailes_-_Top_-_Ruth_Meets_Boaz_as_she_gleans_(Ruth_2_-4-16)_-_Walters_W10618R_-_Full_Page.jpg.

Section Questions

1. List the three vulnerable groups of people that God commands the Israelites to take of in (Exodus 22:21-22; Deuteronomy 24:19-21).

Typology

According to multiple Church Fathers, Boaz's respectful love for and marriage with Ruth prefigures Christ's love for and marriage with His Church. Chrysostom teaches, "Those things which happened to Ruth should be seen as figures. For she was an outsider and had fallen into extreme penury; but Boaz, seeing her, did not despise her on account of her poverty, nor was he horrified on account of her impiety; even as Christ received the church, who was both a stranger and laboring, in need of great good things."[19]

In the first case, Ruth becomes a member of the Israel of old by joining herself to Boaz in marriage where the two "become one flesh (Genesis 2:24 *RSVCE*)." In the latter, by their baptism into Christ's body, Christians are members of the new Israel. Paul relates baptism to a wedding by describing a wedding as "a great mystery, and I mean in reference to Christ and the Church (Ephesians 5:32 *RSVCE*)."

Isidore of Seville, observes, that the Ruth's incorporation into the assembly of Israel by marriage anticipates the time of Christianity when many gentiles will be brought into the assembly of the new

[19] Franke, 190. *Homilies on the Gospel of Matthew* 3 is cited, "MEIT (Ruth), 35*; PG 57: 35-36."

Israel, the Church.[20] Isidore also portrays the Israelite man who withdrew his right to marry Ruth by taking off his sandal and giving it to Boaz as prefiguring John the Baptist who was only a friend of the groom, not the groom himself, and who deemed himself not even worthy to untie the sandal of the bridegroom (John 1:27).[21]

Ruth married Boaz and in time gave birth to Obed. Both Obed and his father Boaz are referred to as a redeemer, in Hebrew *go'el* (גֹּאֵל Ruth 3:12, 4:14). Boaz acted as a kinsman-redeemer. A kinsman-redeemer had various duties that all centered around fulfilling duties that his closest male relative is unable to fulfill, including redeeming a kinsman from slavery, redeeming property of a kinsman, and rearing children of his kinsman if the kinsman died, all as signs of God the ultimate redeemer (Leviticus 25:48-49; Numbers 5:8; Deuteronomy 25:5-6; Joshua 20:5; Isaiah 41:14, 59:20). Boaz demonstrated protective loyalty to his family and kinsmen by redeeming property of Elimelech (Ruth 4:3), and by marrying Elimelech's widow Ruth. Boaz's multiple acts of redemption are inherited by his son,[22] Obed who in turn passes down the redemption to subsequent generations including David, and, finally to Christ, the ultimate redeemer. Jesus visibly showed forth God as the divine redeemer (Isaiah 41:14).

As redeemer Christ fulfills all the previous ways of redemption. As John Paul II teaches, "His silences, His miracles, His gestures, His

---

[20] Franke, 188. *On Ruth* is cited, "MEIT (Ruth), 7-8."

[21] Franke, 188. *On Ruth* is cited, "MEIT (Ruth), 7."; Bergsma and Pitre, 349.

[22] William A. Anderson, *Liguori Catholic Bible Study, Historical Books I: Joshua, Judges, Ruth, 1 and 2 Samuel* (Liguori Catholic Bible Study (Liguori: Liguori Publications, 2013), Kindle location, 1365.

prayer, His love for people, His special affection for the little and the poor, His acceptance of the total sacrifice on the cross for the redemption of the world, and His resurrection are the actualization of His word and the fulfillment of Revelation."[23] Christ is the redeemer in a similar but also different way than all the redeemers of the Old Testament, especially when redeemers were redeemers of blood.

One duty of the redeemer was to be a *go'el ha-dam* (גֹּאֵל הַדָּם), an "avenger of blood (Numbers 35:19 *RSVCE*)." This duty was acquired if one of his kinsmen was killed by person. As an avenger of blood, the redeemer was to search out the killer and kill him. The only place that a killer was safe was one of the six, designated cities of refuge overseen by Levitical priests and only if the killer had killed unintentionally (Numbers 19:4-10, 35:6).

Christ transformed the role of the redeemer of blood by offering his own blood to the Father for our salvation, for our redemption from sin and death. In writing on Christ as the unique redeemer, Benedict XVI states, "When in Matthew's account, the 'whole people' say: 'His blood be on us and on our children' (27 : 25) , the Christian will remember that Jesus ' blood speaks a different language from the blood of Abel (Heb. 12 : 24): it does not cry out for vengeance and punishment; it brings reconciliation. It is not poured out against anyone; it is poured out for many, for all. 'All have sinned and fall short of the glory of God . . . God put [Jesus] forward as an expiation by his

---

[23] John Paul II, "Apostolic Exhortation Catechesi Tradendae, October 16, 1979," w2.vatican.va, http://w2.vatican.va/content/john-paul-ii/en/apost_exhortations/documents/hf_jp-ii_exh_16101979_catechesi-tradendae.html.

blood' (Rom 3: 23, 25)."[24]

Section Questions

1. According to Chrysostom, how does Boaz relationship with Ruth specifically anticipate Jesus' relationship with women?

2. How is Boaz a redeemer and how does Jesus transform the redeemer of blood? Include in your response the following: Ruth, Kinsman-Redeemer, Redeemer of Blood

---

[24] Benedict XVI Joseph Ratzinger, *Faith and Politics Selected Writings*, trans. Michael J. Miller (San Francisco: Ignatius Press, 2018), Kindle Location, 546-548. The following is cited, "From Joseph Ratzinger / Pope Benedict XVI, *Jesus von Nazareth: Zweiter Teil: Vom Einzug in salem bis zur Auferstehung* (Vatican City: Libreria Editrice Vaticana, 2011). Translated by Philip J. Whitmore as *Jesus of Nazareth: Holy Week: From the Entrance into Jerusalem to the Resurrection* (San Francisco: Ignatius Press, 2011), 183-202." (Genesis 4:10; Numbers 19:4-10, 35:19, 6; Hebrews 12:24)

1 Samuel and 2 Samuel

Introduction

The Book of Ruth, which, according to its opening verses, describe events that take place at the end of the time of the Judges, is followed by two books: 1 Samuel and 2 Samuel. These latter books describe the time of the last Judge, Samuel and Israel's first two kings, Saul and David. We will study these books by focusing on a few central people of the book: Hannah, Samuel, Saul, and David.

Hannah

The First Book of Samuel begins by introducing Hannah's husband, Elkanah. According to the first verses of chapter one, Elkanah had two wives: Peninnah who "had children (1 Samuel 1:2 *RSVCE*)" and Hannah who was childless. When Elkanah goes up for his yearly visit to worship at the Shiloh sanctuary of Samaria (Judges 21:19) he is accompanied by Peninnah and Hannah. (Not until King David did Jerusalem become the capital of a united Israel and center for worship (2 Samuel 4:9).)

At the Shiloh sanctuary, Hannah so intensely prays for a child that the priest Eli thinks she is drunk, but she assures Eli that she is not. Then Eli, inspired by God, assures her that God will grant her request, and God does so. After Elkinah returns back home at Ramah, he has relations with Hannah; she conceives and bears a son whom she names Samuel. She brings Samuel to the sanctuary of Shiloh and leaves him there since she had made a promise that if she bears a son she will "give him to the Lord all the days of his life (1 Samuel 1:11 *RSVCE*)."

[1]

The following chapter begins with "Hannah's prayer," which resembles the Magnificat of Mary (Luke 1:46-55). Hannah's prayer, according to Bergsma and Pitre, sets the tone for the entire books of Samuel in particular the theme of rise and fall, of God raising the lowly, and humbling the proud. Often the lowly person who is raised and the person who is humbled is the same person, as we will see in lives of Samuel, Saul and David. We will see this played out first with Samuel, and afterwards in the lives of Saul and David where, borrowing from a phrase attributed to Mark Twain, history does not repeat itself

---

[1] Julius Schnorr von Carolsfeld [Public domain], "Hannah's prayer, 1860 woodcut by Julius Schnorr von Karolsfeld," https://commons.wikimedia.org/wiki/File:Schnorr_von_Carolsfeld_Bibel_in_Bildern_1860_086.png.

exactly but rather contains patterns that rhyme. One identifiable pattern in salvation history that providential rhymes, is the rising of the lowly, the lowly gaining power and then being humbled.

Before doing so, it is important to note that Hannah's rise from the lowliness of barrenness to the greatness of giving birth to a prophet-judge, Samuel, is traditionally understood as a foreshadowing of Mary's rise from lowliness and exaltation as Mother of God. Due to Mary's sinlessness, God never needed to humble her in her exalted state. She remained humble throughout her life despite being the Mother of Jesus, the Mother of God.

Another distinguishing feature of Mary is that unlike the barren and then fertile Old Testament women who foreshadowed her, (Sarah, Rebekah, Rachel, and Hannah), Mary was fertile while remaining a virgin. Commenting on this difference the Hans Urs von Balthasar notes that "the decisive appearance of God as the sole Father … excludes a relation to another father…."[2] for in the New Testament, "[t]he whole process of bodily begetting, in fact, the whole question of whether a man or woman is [physically] fruitful or not, loses its importance."[3]

Section Questions

1. How does Hannah foreshadow Mary? Include the following in your response: Magnificat (Luke 1:46-55), Humble, Proud, Barren, Fertility, Faith, Samuel's Dedication

---

[2] Joseph Ratzinger, Hans Urs von Balthasar, trans. A. Walker *Mary: the Church at the Source* (San Francisco: Ignatius Press, 2005), 152.

[3] Ratzinger, 152.

Samuel

Hannah gave her firstborn son the name Samuel because, she says, "I have asked him of the Lord (1 Samuel 1:20 *RSVCE*)." The Hebrew word for Samuel, *Shemuel* (שְׁמוּאֵל), is made up of two Hebrew words *shem* (שֵׁם), meaning name, and *el* (אֵל) referring to God.[4] It could, in addition, be a defined by the Hebrew root *shema*, (שָׁמַע) hear, and *el*, God. As interpreted in the latter manner, Hannah names her son Samuel because she has been heard by God.

[5]

[4] "8050. Shemuel, Strong's Concordance, NAS Exhaustive Concordance," biblehub.com, https://biblehub.com/hebrew/8050.htm. "8086. Shema, Strong's Concordance," biblehub.com, https://biblehub.com/hebrew/8086.htm.

[5] Frank William Warwick Topham [Public domain], "Samuel Dedicated by Hannah at the Temple by Frank W.W. Topham,"

In a vision, God tells the young Samuel that the high priest of Shiloh, Eli, and Eli's two sons will be punished because of the blasphemy committed by the sons and the failure of Eli to correct his son. With respect to Eli's sin of omission, of Eli's failure to correct his sons John Chrysostom warns:

> Hence, I beg you to offer a hand to our children lest we ourselves become liable for what is committed by them. Are you not aware of what happened to old Eli for not properly correcting his son's shortcomings? I mean, when a disease requires surgery, it rapidly becomes incurable if the physician is bent on treating it with skin ointments and does not apply the appropriate remedy. In just the same way it behooved that old man to take appropriate action regarding his sons' failing, but by being excessive tolerance he too shared in their punishment." Eli and his two sons are punished by tragic, humiliating deaths and Samuel rises in prominence both as a prophet and as a judge.[6]

Samuel also, will be humbled by God after being raised to level of great prominence among the Israelites. This occurs when God accommodates the Israelites request to have a king, and, thereby rejecting Samuel's leadership over them as judge and Samuel's two

---

https://commons.wikimedia.org/wiki/File:Samuel_dedicated_by_Hannah.jpg.

[6] John R. Franke, *Ancient Christian Commentary on Scripture: Old Testament IV, Joshua, Judges, Ruth, 1-2 Samuel* (Downers Grove: Intervarsity Press, 2014) 228. The following is cited, "*Homilies on Genesis* 59.20".

sons whom, in his old age, he had appointed as judges (1 Samuel 8:1). A reason that the people rejected his son's as judges was that they did not live an upright life as their father did. Instead they had "turned after gain" accepting brides and "pervert[ing] justice (1 Samuel 8:3 *RSVCE*)." In reaction, the Israelites insist that Samuel "appoint for us a king to govern us like all the nations (1 Samuel 8:5 *RSVCE*)." Already, in Deuteronomy this Israelite desire for a king was anticipated, "When you come to the land which the Lord your God gives you, and you possess it and dwell in it, and then say, 'I will set a king over me, like all the nations that are round about me'; you may indeed set as king over you him whom the Lord your God will choose. (Deuteronomy 17:14 *RSVCE*)."

This is precisely what takes place; after dwelling in the Promised Land for a number of generations the Israelites want to be like the other nations who are ruled by a powerful king. Deuteronomy, though, instructs the Israelites that when they establish a king over themselves that the following conditions are met. First, the king must be a fellow Israelite. Second, the king must not "multiply horses (Deuteronomy 17:16 *RSVCE*)." This means, interprets Pitre, not to amass a large army that has many horses since God is to be the primary source of Israelite strength.[7] In addition, the Israelite king may not marry multiple women, nor may he accumulate vast quantities of silver and gold, since, once again God is to be the king's primary treasure. Chapter seventeen ends by commanding the future Israelite kings to read these laws "all the days of his life (Deuteronomy 17:19 *RSVCE*)" so as not to forget proper fear of the Lord. Sadly, these laws

---

[7] Brant Pitre, *The Old Testament-A Historical and Theological Journey through Jewish Scripture*, MP 3 21.

were repeatedly broken by the kings of Israel, who were also at times encouraged by their own people to break them due to the Israelite's disordered lack of trust in God as their strength and excessive trust in a strong king.

Angered by the Israelite's request for a king, Samuel turns to prayer and in prayer God reminds Samuel that the people are not rejecting his leadership but rather by wanting to have a king like other nations the people are rejecting God's kingship over them, and their role, as Bergsma and Pitre state, of being God's "firstborn son (Exodus 4:22 *RSVCE*)," with the responsibility of leading as a kingdom of priests all other people to worship of the true God.[8] Rejecting this role and God's providential care for them, the Israelites insist on being like other people who place their trust in an earthly king "who will go out before us and fight our battles 1 Samuel 8:20 *RSVCE*)." God concedes to their request, but before doing so he has Samuel to warn the Israelites that if they a king is appointed for them the king will tax, enroll them into the military, and enslave them. (1 Samuel 8:11-17) Humbly, Samuel obeys and soon afterwards anoints Israel's first king, Saul.

Bergsma and Pitre, further add that although God allows the Israelites to reject him as their king and turn their back on their priestly leadership role as first-born among the nations, God does not in turn reject the Israelites. Instead, God patiently and subtlety re-directs Israel's misguided choices by eventually reconciling the Israelites choice of an earthly king with their vocation to be a priestly people who lead all the nations to God as king. The perfect fulfillment

---

[8] John Bergsma and Brant Pitre, *A Catholic Introduction to the Bible, Volume I* (San Francisco: Ignatius Press, 2018), 358.

of this reconciliation is anticipated in King David who at times assumes a priestly role (1 Samuel 21:6; 2 Samuel 6:14, 17).

Finally, in fulfillment of a prophecy of Micah, the reconciliation perfectly occurs at the Incarnation when Jesus, the Divine King, the Son of God, takes on flesh at Bethlehem, King's David's town. "But you, O Bethlehem Ephrathah, who are little to be among the clans of Judah, from you shall come forth from me one who is to be ruler in Israel, whose origin is from old, from ancient days (Micah 5:2 *RSVCE*)." Through Jesus, explains Bergsma and Pitre, a New Israel is formed that is not ethnically based but, as Catholic, as pertaining to the whole, is open to all people and invites all people from all nations to participate in Christ's kingship and priesthood.

> Come to him, to that living stone, rejected by men but in God's sigh chosen and precious; and like living stones be yourselves built into a spiritual house, to be a holy priesthood, to offer spiritual sacrifices acceptable to God through Jesus Christ… you are a chosen race, a royal priesthood, a holy nation, God's own nation (1 Peter 2:4, 9 *RSVCE*).[9]

Section Questions

1. In a specific sense, how did Eli and Samuel both similarly treat their sons?

2. According to Deuteronomy specifically what are the three conditions that God wants Israelite kings to follow and why?

---

[9] Bergsma and Pitre, 372.

Saul

The first king that Samuel anoints is Saul of the house of Benjamin. As he was being chosen by God through Samuel, Saul acknowledges his lowly status with, "Am I not a Benjaminite, from the least of the tribes of Israel? And is not my family the humblest of all the families of the tribe of Benjamin (1 Samuel 9:21 *RSVCE*)?" As the Book of Judges depicts, the tribe of Benjamin is the lowliest of tribes because they were held responsible for the terrible immoral act of raping the concubine of Levite (Judges 19:25). In response, the remaining tribes of Israel fought the tribe of Benjamin, and, in so doing, almost killed every member (Judges 20). Providentially, a few remained and with the aid of the other tribes it remained intact but at a greatly reduced number and with a tarnished reputation. Despite the reputation of the tribe of Benjamin, God chooses from their lowly state one to rule as king over all of Israel, Saul.

Saul fulfills the expectation of his people by courageously defending them from their enemies and defeating many of Israel's enemies, including the Ammonites, Moabites, Edomites, Philistines, and Amalekites. He was so successful in battle that 1 Samuel states, "he fought against all his enemies on every side…wherever he turned he put them to worse (1 Samuel 14:47 *RSVCE*)." God enhanced Saul's effective leadership by blessing Saul with the gift of prophecy much to the surprise of Saul's people (1 Samuel 10:9-13).

Tragically, Saul became sinfully proud of his victories and blessings. In time, he became so proud that he even disobeyed an explicit command from God (1 Samuel 15), was repeatedly unfaithful to God and, consequently, fell out of favor with God who rejects him as King. Speaking on behalf of God, Samuel tells Saul "the Lord has rejected you from being king over Israel. … The Lord has torn the kingdom of Israel from you this day, and has given it to a neighbor of yours, who is better than you (1 Samuel 15:26-28 *RSVCE*)."

[10]

Saul's sins, points out William A. Anderson, did not hurt himself alone,[11] for personal sin have social repercussions as the Catechism teaches, "thus sin makes men accomplices of one another and causes concupiscence, violence, and injustice to reign among them. Sins give rise to social situations and institutions that are contrary to the divine goodness. 'Structures of sin' are the expression and effect of personal sins. They lead their victims to do evil in their turn. In an analogous

[10] Rembrandt or workshop [Public domain], "Saul and David by Rembrandt Mauritshuis 621," https://commons.wikimedia.org/wiki/File:Saul_and_David_by_Rembrandt_Mauritshuis_621.jpg.

[11] William A. Anderson, *Ligouri Catholic Bible Study, Historical Books I: Joshua, Judges, Ruth, 1 and 2 Samuel* (Ligouri: Ligouri Publications, 2013), Kindle location 1982.

sense, they constitute a 'social sin.' (*CCC* 1869)"[12]

The social consequences of Saul's sin are especially in the last battle he fought against the Philistines (1 Samuel 31). During this battle the Philistines killed not only Saul but also his three sons, including Jonathan. According to 1 Chronicles the reason that Saul lost was because God had abandoned him due to Saul's failure to "keep the command of the Lord…Therefore the Lord slew him [through the Philistines] and turned the kingdom over to David (1 Chronicles 10:13-14 *RSVCE*)."

Section Questions

1. What tribe did King Saul come from, and what tribe did King David come from?

David

David like Saul, but with a very important difference, was raised from a lowly state to the greatness of a king and then, due to pride, greatly displeased God, and suffered from the consequences of his sinful actions which also reverberated in history. We will begin with his rise from lowliness.

David's father was Jesse of the tribe of Judah. Jesse, in turn, was the son of Obed, who was the son of Boaz, and Ruth, whose life we reflected upon previously. Of Jesse's eight sons, David was the youngest and, consequently, deemed socially least important among

---

[12] "Catechism of the Catholic Church, no. 1869" vatican.va, http://www.vatican.va/archive/ccc_css/archive/catechism/p3s1c1a8.htm.

his brothers, and yet, through Samuel, God chose David to the new king of Israel. God's choice of David surprised not only the David's family but also Samuel who began with the oldest son (1 Chronicles 2:13) as a possible candidate that God would choose to be king, but God told Samuel, "I have rejected him (1 Samuel 16:7 *RSVCE*)."

[13]

Afterwards, Jesse has the rest of his sons, except for David, present themselves to Samuel, but once again God rejects all of them. Finally, David, who was considered so lowly that he was not even invited is called from tending sheep and is presented before Samuel. Upon being

---

[13] Pollard, Josephine, 1834-1892. [from old catalog] [No restrictions], "David raises the head of Goliath as illustrated by Josephine Pollard (1899)," https://commons.wikimedia.org/wiki/File:Sweet_stories_of_God;_in_the_language_of_childhood_and_the_beautiful_delineations_of_sacred_art_(1899)_(14751566596).jpg.

presented to Samuel, God says to Samuel "Arise, anoint him (1 Samuel 16:12 *RSVCE*)" as king.

David's defeat of Goliath, the Philistine giant, with but a stone thrown from a slingshot well represents David's astonishing rise from lowliness to greatness. This meteoric rise, though, did not come without overcoming obstacles, which at times included fighting, as evident in his one-to-one fight with Goliath. With respect to God calling David to greatness while, at the same time, providentially arranging David's gradual ascent through difficulties and over obstacles, Andersen observes, "When God chooses someone for some particular task in creation, God does not necessarily remove all obstacles hindering the fulfillment of God's plan."[14] And, we can add, that the obstacles themselves might serve as steps in God's plan leading to a particular divinely willed end, such as kingship in the case of David.

Upon taking the throne and being recognized by the people of Israel as their legitimate king, David begins to rule. David ruled in a noble, upright virtuous manner, but, sadly, like Saul, allows the power of his office to become a force for evil, and in the process he hurts himself and many others, most notably Uriah the Hittite whom, after David commits adultery with Uriah's wife Bathsheba, orders to be sent in the frontlines of a battle to be killed. In warning against such abuses of power that all office holders face, and not just Saul and David, Pope Francis said, "Please, allow me to say it loud and clear: the more powerful you are, the more your actions will have an impact on people,

---

[14] William A. Anderson, *Ligouri Catholic Bible Study, Historical Books I: Joshua, Judges, Ruth, 1 and 2 Samuel* (Ligouri: Ligouri Publications, 2013), Kindle location 2058.

the more responsible you are to act humbly. If you don't, your power will ruin you, and you will ruin the other. There is a saying in Argentina: 'Power is like drinking gin on an empty stomach.' You feel dizzy, you get drunk, you lose your balance, and you will end up hurting yourself and those around you, if you don't connect your power with humility and tenderness."[15]

The cascade of sin that David experiences takes place at the very height of his power when he has demonstrated fidelity to God, faithfulness to the covenant God established with him.[16] At this height

---

[15] "Pope Francis' 'Talk' to TED (Full Text), April 26, 2017," zenit.org, https://zenit.org/articles/pope-francis-talk-to-ted-full-text/.

[16] John Bergsma and Brant Pitre, *A Catholic Introduction to the Bible, Volume I* (San Francisco: Ignatius Press, 2018), 365. Bergsma and Pitre explain, "although the word 'covenant' is not used in Nathan's oracle to David, several aspects strongly suggest it is implied. For one thing, the father-and-son language (2 Sam 7:14) is covenantal insofar as it establishes a divine family. Moreover, God's promise to give David a 'great name' (2 Sam 7:9) is a direct echo of the promise of a 'great name' (= royalty) that was given to Abraham (Gen 12:2) and incorporated into the second stage of the Abrahamic covenant (see Gen 17:4-6). By means of this allusion, the sacred author shows that the promise to Abraham 'kings shall come forth from you' will find its ultimate fulfillment in the kingdom promised to David and his heirs. Last, but not certainly not least, not only do parallel texts in the Psalms make explicit that a covenant was formed with David by this oracle (Ps 89:19-37; 132:1-18), but the book of Samuel itself ends by interpreting this event as establishing a covenant: 'The oracle of David, the son of Jesse . . . the anointed of the God of Jacob, the sweet psalmist of Israel. . . . [D]oes not my house stand so with God? For he has made with me an everlasting covenant, ordered in all things and secure' (2 Sam 23:1, 5)."

and acclaim by the Israelites, observers Bergsma and Pitre, David falls by staying away from battle, falling into laziness, and in his sloth allowing his eyes to wander,[17] until one day a noon, the time of day when we often are most tempted to sloth, he is tempted by the "Noonday Devil"[18]. Tempted, David lustfully gazes upon the beautiful woman Bathsheba who is washing (*rachats* רָחַץ) herself (2 Samuel 11:2). Often, comments Miller, the Hebrew word, *rachats* (רָחַץ), is translated as bathing. Miller maintains that translating the Hebrew word as bathing is not a good translation since every other time the word is used in the Old Testament it is translated as washing not bathing. The word bathing bears with it the unjustified connotation that Bathsheba could have been enticing David into sin as she bathed naked. Instead, the original Hebrew text, argues Miller, indicates that:

> She's washing; she's washing on the rooftop, because if you want hot water you leave it in a tank up on the roof in the hot sun of the Middle East, and that way you have hot water to wash with. There's no indication that she's naked at all. And I'll point out that the text says, "David sent messengers and took her." There's no volition on her part. No decision on her part. The king says: you come. And: "When she came to him, he took her to bed." There's no indication that he even speaks to her. So, far from being the seductress, Bathsheba is if anything a victim of a rape.[19]

---

[17] Bergsma and Brant Pitre, 365.

[18] Cf. Psalm 91:6 "the destruction that wastes at noonday (RSV)."

[19] Robert D. Miller II, *Understanding the Old Testament* (Chantilly: The Teaching Company, 2019), 193.

Lustfully watching Bathsheba innocently wash herself, David chooses to disorderly possess her for himself despite her being married to another man. After ordering her to be brought to him, and raping her David sinks even further into vice and becomes responsible for indirectly murdering Bathsheba's husband, Uriah the Hittite, so that Uriah does not find out that the child Bathsheba has conceived is not his but rather is King David's.

[20]

Bergsma and Pitre also comment that David's sins have a terrible social affect as his own family commit similar sins including David's son Amnon who, resembling his father, seizes a beautiful woman, his

---

[20] James Tissot / Public domain, "desolation of Tamar," https://commons.wikimedia.org/wiki/File:Desolation_of_Tamar_by_J.Tissot.jpg.

half-sister Tamar, who he desires for himself and then violently rapes her. This, like a chain reaction, leads to Tamar's brother Absalom, who also is David's son, to avenge his sister's rape by murdering his brother Amnon (2 Samuel 13:29) along with all his other brothers.[21] Eventually King David forgives Absalom but then Absalom responds not by repenting but rather by trying to seize the throne for himself and steal the people's loyalty away from his father. One way he does this is by sending out messengers throughout Israel to announce that "Absalom is king (2 Samuel 15:10 *RSVCE*)" and then by publicly having sexual relations with King David's concubines on the roof of the royal palace (2 Samuel 16:22), the precise place that David, points out Hahn, lustfully watched Bathsheba bathe.[22]

As Scripture teaches David sowed evil, including adultery and murder, which in time he experienced done unto him, even after he had repented since the evil had already been sown in history. David experienced the consequences of his sins by his sons being murdered and his concubines being raped in public by one of his sons. As Galatians states, "for whatever a man sows, that he will also reap (Galatians 6:7 *RSVCE*)." Similarly, the Book of Proverbs teaches "they shall eat the fruit of their way (1:31 *RSVCE*)." "The iniquities of the wicked ensnare him and he is caught in the toils of his sin (5:22 *RSVCE*)." "He who sows injustice will reap calamity, and the rod of his fury will fail (22:8 *RSVCE*)."

Along with teaching that evildoers often experience the evil they do unto others, Scripture also teaches that doing good encourages the

---

[21] Bergsma and Pitre, 174.

[22] Scott Hahn and Curtis Mitch, *The First and Second Book of Samuel* (San Francisco: Ignatius Press, 2016), loc. 5150.

growth of goodness in others that we likely will also experience. "He who has a bountiful eye will be blessed…He who loves purity of heart, and whose speech is gracious, will have the king as his friend (Proverbs 22:9, 11 *RSVCE*)." Like Job, and ultimately like Christ, we may do good and not experience goodness done unto us in this life but Christ assure us that as often as we did good to "one of the least of these my brethren (Matthew 25:40 *RSVCE*)" we did unto Christ, our King with the hope that he will bless us with the goodness of everlasting life. We will see how the good that David did established precedents for future good.

One way that David sowed seeds of goodness that were reaped, observes Bergsma and Pitre, for around 400 years was his refusal to kill Saul when he had the opportunity. "The Lord forbid" swears David "that I should do this thing to my lord, the Lord's anointed, to put forth my hand against him (1 Samuel 24:6 *RSVCE*)." This noble decision of David, had the effect, writes Bergsma and Pitre, of establishing "a political precedent in Judah that helped foster a culture opposed to assassination and civil war. As a result, David's dynasty ruled for about 400 years: the longest-lived dynasty in the ancient Near East."[23] Another essential way that David was good even during his moments of moral depravity was by never worshipping false gods liturgically as his son Solomon repeatedly did. This fidelity in worship is later used as a standard, explains Hahn, by which all other kings are judged by, as is evident when King Abijam is described as having a "heart not wholly true to the Lord his God, as the heart of David his father (1 Kings 15:3 *RSVCE*)" since Abijam, like King Rehoboam who

[23] Bergsma and Pitre, 361.

preceded him, worshipped false Gods.[24]

[25]

From a Catholic perspective, all the good that David did and represents is fulfilled in Jesus. This manner of perceiving David as fulfilled in Jesus is affirmed by Jesus in his explanation to Pharisees who question his and his disciples' action of eating heads of grain on the Sabbath. Jesus responds, "Haven't you read what David did when he and his companions were hungry? He entered the house of God, and he and his companions ate the consecrated bread—which was not

---

[24] *Ignatius Catholic Study Bible, The First and Second Book of Kings, Commentary, Notes, & Study Questions, Revised Standard Version, Second Catholic Edition, with Introduction, Commentary, and Notes by Scott Hahn, and Curtis Mitch* (San Francisco: Ignatius Press, 2017), Kindle location 2435.

[25] Gustave Doré [Public domain], "David mourning the death of Absalom, by Gustave Doré," https://commons.wikimedia.org/wiki/File:081.David_Mourns_the_Death_of_Absalom.jpg.

lawful for them to do, but only for the priests (Matthew 12:3-4 *RSVCE*)."

Among typological comparisons of the Church Fathers between David and Jesus are the following. St. Augustine, sees the kingship that was passed from the old King Saul to the new King David, who acted both as a king and priest, as fulfilled in Christ as "the eternal priest-king."[26] Church Fathers see the "eternal" (2 Samuel 6:13) aspect of the kingdom of David as fulfilled in the Kingdom God represented by the Catholic Church on earth in a present but not yet perfected manner, this will only take place at the end of time, when all of creation, including time will be transformed (Revelation 21:1).

For St. Augustine, not only is David's kingdom a shadow of the future Kingdom Jesus would establish through his Church on earth but also "the kingdom of Saul himself, who certainly was reprobated and rejected, was the shadow of a kingdom yet to come which should remain to eternity."[27] Augustine adds that David's and his son Solomon's international influence and power over surrounding nations is fulfilled by the birth of Jesus who begins on earth in a visible way what David's and Solomon's kingdom anticipated.[28] The Church is the visible presence of the eternal kingdom of heaven by being, in

---

[26] Hahn and Mitch, loc. 2032. The following is cited, "St Augustine, *City of God* 17,4)".

[27] Augustine, "The City of God (Book XVII), Chap. 6," newadvent.org, http://www.newadvent.org/fathers/120117.htm.

[28] Augustine, "The City of God (Book XVII), Chap. 2," newadvent.org, http://www.newadvent.org/fathers/120117.htm.

the words of Hahn, a "Sacramental Society."[29] In this society, all people from all nations are offered the possibility of experiencing the heavenly kingdom through the Seven Sacraments but not in a definite manner. This will only be experienced by God's grace after one death.

The universal nature of David's kingdom and later, more intensely, in Solomon's kingdom is not the only way that the Old Testament prepares for the universal, eternal kingdom of God that the Catholic Church sacramentally is a presence of. God prepares for the universal (Catholic) Church in multiple ways throughout the Old Testament. To name just a few, in Genesis God is presented as the father creator of all people. After two notable falls into evil by Adam and Eve and, after Noah a New Adam, Benedict XVI explains that God calls all the nations gradually back to himself by electing one nation, Israel (and more precisely one man, Jacob who is renamed Israel and who is the father of the Twelve Tribes) for the salvation of all nations. Before, choosing Jacob, God calls Abram who he promises to bless all nations through (Genesis 12:3). Israel's role of leading the other nations to the one God becomes clearer with Israel being called the "first-born son (Exodus 4:22 *RSVCE*)" and a "kingdom of priests (Exodus 19:6 *RSVCE*)."

As Hahn explains, the first-born son is to set an example for all his brothers and sisters by leading them by example. Furthermore, before the establishment of the Levitical priesthood after Israel's sin of worshipping the golden calf, the priesthood was simply the privilege of first-born sons, due to the expectation that these first-born sons are

---

[29] Scott Hahn, *The First Society: The Sacrament of Matrimony and the Restoration of the Social Order* (Steubenville: Emmaus Road Publishing, 2018), Kindle location 1936 of 2196.

to be models.[30] Later, the Prophet Isaiah, will strongly reaffirm the universal reason for Israel's particular election by repeatedly describing Israel's role of leading all nations back to God. Among other ways, Isaiah uses the image of Israel being a guiding light for other nations (42:6; 49:6; 60:3).[31]

Virtues that David excelled in also find their fulfillment in Jesus Christ in particular David's faithfulness, generosity, and humility. By shedding his innocent blood for our salvation, Jesus's surpasses David's generosity. Similarly, by being "obedient unto death, even death on a cross (Philippians 2:8 *RSVCE*)" Jesus fulfills David's imperfect obedience, and by perfectly representing in these actions God's faithfulness to his covenant's Jesus fulfills David's faithfulness.

The Davidic characteristic of faithfulness merits more attention since it is a key biblical term. Bergsma and Pitre define the faithfulness, the *chesed* (חֶסֶד) that David practiced, as "covenant fidelity: the loyalty, love and mercy expected between covenant partners."[32] The greatest example of covenant fidelity is God, who always is faithful, despite the repeated failings of partners he enters into relationship with. David images this surprising fidelity of God in a number of noble ways including refusing to harm Saul even when he was twice in the position to end Saul's life when Saul was seeking to kill David (1 Samuel 24:4-6; 26:11).

---

[30] Scott Hahn, *Catholic Bible Dictionary* (New York: Doubleday, 2009), 725. Hahn references Job 1:5 as representative of patriarchal priesthood where fathers were naturally priests of their families.

[31] Joseph Ratzinger, *The Meaning of Christian Brotherhood* (San Francisco: Ignatius Press, 1993, 8.

[32] Bergsma and Pitre, 353.

Bergsma and Pitre point out that another notable way that David demonstrated covenant fidelity to King Saul, is evident in the first chapter of 2 Samuel, which describes David's reaction to a messenger who reports that Saul has been killed. David responds not be rejoicing, but rather by mourning, tearing his clothes, fasting, and praising Saul as one of "the mighty fallen (2 Samuel 1:19 *RSVCE*)."[33] David's noble action in relationship to Saul is surpassed by Christ who on the cross does not condemn us for crucifying him but rather asks his Father, "forgive them; for they know not what they do (Luke 23:34 *RSVCE*)." The ignorance of his executioners, explains Ron Rolheiser, was not knowing "how much they are loved." In other words, not knowing how faithful God is in his covenant relationships even when God is rejected in terrible ways. Rolheiser continues describing Jesus' *chesed* that surpasses King David's with:

> Jesus was capable of continuing to love and forgive in the face of hatred and murder because, at the very heart of his self-awareness, lay an awareness of who he was, God's son, and how much he was loved. He wasn't thick-skinned or elitist, just in touch with who he was and how much he was loved. From that source he drew his energy and his power to forgive. We too have access to that same powerful spring of energy. Like Jesus, we too are God's children and are loved that deeply. Like Jesus, we too can be that forgiving.[34]

---

[33] Bergsma and Pitre, 362.

[34] Ron Rolheiser, "Love in a Time of Opposition," July 25, 2010, ronrolheiser.com, http://ronrolheiser.com/love-in-a-time-of-opposition/

Not only is Jesus prefigured in the books of Samuel by David, but Jesus' mother Mary is also foreshadowed, principally as the New Ark, the bearer, of the New Covenant, who is her son Jesus. As explained by Hahn, according to Exodus and Deuteronomy, since the ark was so holy it was to be born in a special manner, specifically by being carefully carried with poles that rested on the shoulders of a team of Levites (Exodus 25:14; Deuteronomy 10:8). These explicit directions that helped to ensure that the ark would not fall were disregarded when David ordered the ark to be brought from Abinadab's house to Jerusalem. The holy contents of the ark were the Ten Commandments, Aaron's rod, and an urn of manna (Hebrews 9:4). Instead of carefully carrying the ark, Abinadab's sons, Uzzah and Ahio, drive by oxen to Jerusalem on a cart. When the ox trip and cause the ark to fall, Uzzah reaches out to prevent the fall and upon touching the ark is struck dead by God (2 Samuel 6:7).[35]

Another way that the ark is indicated as holy, because of its contents, was the wood it was made out of. According to Exodus, the ark was made out of acacia (Exodus 25:10). The Jewish first century historian Josephus describes acacia as "naturally strong and could not be corrupted."[36] These details of the ark are fulfilled in Mary who, also because of what, or rather who, she bore, is holy, and, with respect to sin, untouchable and incorruptible. St. Maximus of Turin, points out

---

#.W_NF6S2ZNhF . Rolheiser attributes this explanation of ignorance to Karl Rahner.

[35] Hahn and Mitch, loc. 4739.

[36] Flavius Josephus, "The Antiquities of the Jews," bk. 3, chap. 6, trans. William Whiston, gutenberg.org, http://www.gutenberg.org/files/2848/2848-h/2848-h.htm#link32HCH0006.

Bergsma and Pitre, in interpreting the ark of the Old Testament in reference to the ark of the New Testament writes:

> The prophet David Danced, then. But what would we say that the ark was if not holy Mary, since the ark carried within it the tables of the covenant, while Mary bore the master of the same covenant? The one bore the law within itself and the other the gospel, but the ark gleamed within and without with the radiance of gold while holy Mary shone within and without with the splendor of virginity; the one was adorned with earthly gold, the other with heavenly.[37]

[38]

We will soon end our reflection on the books of Samuel, but before concluding a few words will be offered on the work as a whole.

---

[37] Maximus of Turin, *The Sermons of St. Maximus of Turin*, trans. Boniface Ramsey (New York: Newman Press, 1989), 107. The Sermon cited is Sermon 42; John Bergsma and Brant Pitre, *A Catholic Introduction to the Bible, Volume I* (San Francisco: Ignatius Press, 2018), 377.

[38] J. James Tissot [Public domain], "The Chastisement of Uzzah," https://commons.wikimedia.org/wiki/File:TissUzah.jpg.

As well phrased by Bergsma and Pitre, taken as a whole "the books of Samuel present a literary, historical, and theological masterpiece: a richly textured, realistic, and certainly not sanitized account of the workings of God with human beings, in which God's plans advance sometimes because of, but more often in spite of, the deeds and characters of those with whom God chooses to work."[39]

For Blessed Cardinal Newman this manner of presenting history in its unvarnished, raw state is, sadly, rarely done, including when Church history is written. Newman describes the tendency to tidy up history and present its people in a highly simplified, one dimensional manner as an "endemic perennial fidget which possesses us about giving scandal; facts are omitted in great histories, or glosses are put upon memorable acts, because they are thought not edifying, whereas of all scandals such omissions, such glosses, are the greatest."[40] In another work Newman then describes the history of Christianity in a way that well resembles how God inspired the two books of Samuel to be written in a raw, unsanitized manner:

> But in truth the whole course of Christianity from the first, when we come to examine it, is but one series of troubles and disorders. Every century is like every other, and to those who live in it seems worse than all times before it. The Church is ever ailing, and lingers on in weakness, "always bearing about in the body the dying of the Lord Jesus, that the life also of Jesus might be made manifest in her body." Religion seems

---

[39] Bergsma and Pitre, 356.

[40] John Henry Newman, *Historical Sketches, Vol. 2* (London: Basil Montagu Pickering, 1873), 231.

> ever expiring, schisms dominant, the light of Truth dim, its adherents scattered. The cause of Christ is ever in its last agony, as though it were but a question of time whether it fails finally this day or another. The Saints are ever all but failing from the earth, and Christ all but coming; and thus the Day of Judgment is literally ever at hand; ... "The floods are risen, the floods have lift up their voice, the floods lift up their waves. The waves of the sea are mighty, and rage horribly; but yet the Lord, who dwelleth on high, is mightier [Psalm 93:3-4]."[41]

When we are confronted with the failings of leaders, especially in the Church, may we remember how within significant people in the books of Samuel, including David, Saul, Samuel, and Eli, greatness and vice are interwoven together, and despite the vice of these leaders God still carries out his divine plan of salvation, moving this plan forward, closer to the end of time when one day heaven and earth will fully embrace and earth will be transformed into a new earth where sin is banished once and for all (Revelation 21:1-4).

Section Questions

1. Was David the youngest or oldest of Jesse's sons?

2. According to Bergsma and Pitre, what important political precedent did David establish that helped to bring about the longest lasting dynasty in the Ancient Near East?

---

[41] John Henry Newman, *The Via Media of the Anglican Church, Vol. 1* (London: Basil Montagu Pickering, 1877), 354-355.

3. According to Miller, what does the Hebrew word for washing (*Rachats* רָחַץ) in 2 Samuel 11:2 indicate in how David lusted after Bathsheba. Include the following in your response: Bathing, Nude, Enticing, Rape.

4. How specifically does a sin of Amnon repeat David's sin with Bathsheba and how does help to bring about more sin in David's family? In your response include the following: Tamar, Absalom, Brothers, Concubines, Roof of Palace

5. How did David specifically demonstrate "covenant fidelity (Bergsma:Pitre)" that foreshadowed Jesus' covenant fidelity and how specifically did Jesus' covenant fidelity surpass David's? In your response include the following: Covenant Fidelity to Saul, Jesus on the Cross.

6. How specifically did the Ark foreshadow Mary? Include the following in your response: Contents of Ark and How Mary and Her Child Specifically Fulfills Each One, Ark's Wood

1 Kings and 2 Kings

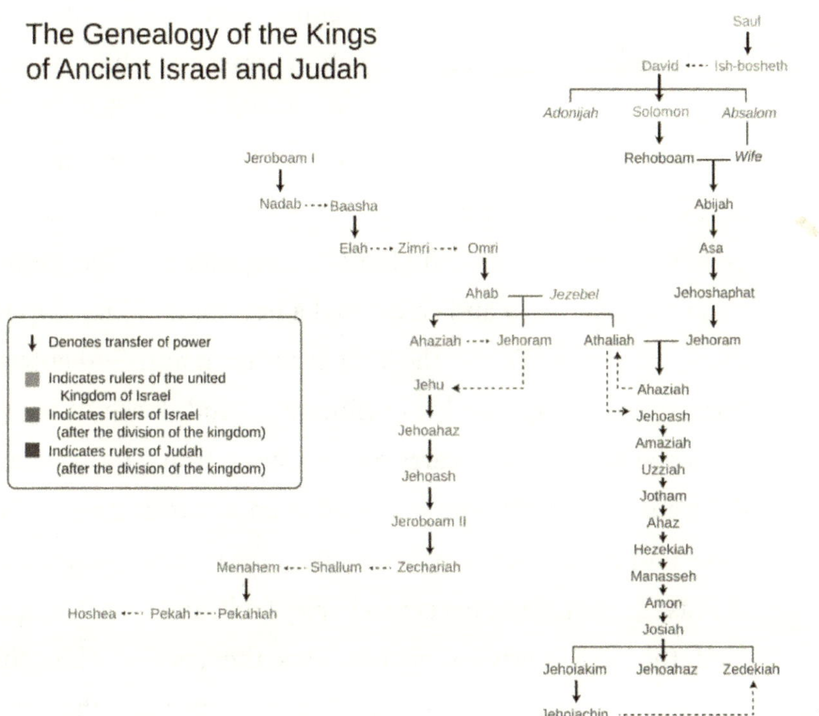

[1]

---

[1] Genealogy_of_the_kings_of_Israel_and_Judah.png: User:Mr. Absurd-derivative work: Jon C [Public domain], "The kings of Israel and Judah" [To adjust for the lack of color, the rulers of the united kingdom are Saul, David, and Solomon (top right); the rulers of Israel, everyone on the left hand column to the left of Jezebel; and the rulers of Judah, everyone on the right hand column below Solomon] https://commons.wikimedia.org/wiki/File:Genealogy_of_the_kings_of_Israel_and_Judah.svg.

Introduction

In commenting on the role of kings in Israelite history, Benedict XVI states:

> It is obvious that God did not intend Israel to have a kingdom. The kingdom was, in fact, a result of Israel's rebellion against God and against his prophets, a defection from the original will of God. The law was to be Israel's king, and, through the law, God himself... But Israel was jealous of the neighboring peoples with their powerful kings... Surprisingly, God yielded to Israel's obstinacy and so devised a new kind of kingship for them. The son of David, the king, is Jesus; in him God entered humanity and espoused it to himself... God does not have a fixed plan that he must carry out; on the contrary, he has many different ways of finding man and even of turning his wrong ways into right ways. We can see that, for instance, in the case of Adam, whose fault became a happy fault, and we see it again in all the twisted ways of history. This, then, is God's kingship – a love that is impregnable and an inventiveness that finds man by ways that are always new.[2]

1 and 2 Kings narrates the history of the Israelite kings whom God graciously permitted to rule but with the intent to gradually convert the rebellious hearts of His people who rejected God's divine kingship in their clamoring "that we also may be like all the nations (1 Samuel

---

[2] Benedict XVI, *Day by Day with Pope Benedict XVI*, ed. Peter John Cameron (San Francisco: Ignatius Press, 2006), 357.

8:20 *RSVCE*)." God subtly, and "sweetly (Wisdom 8:1 *DRA*)" orders human beings back to Himself by allowing the Israelites to be governed by kings, permitting the breakup of a united Davidic Kingdom into two competing kingdoms, overseeing the dissolution of first the Northern Kingdom of Israel and later the Southern Kingdom of Judah, until finally sending his son, Jesus Christ who is a king but, whose "kingship is not from this world (John 18:36 *RSVCE*)" but rather from heaven which one day will be fully united to earth at the end of time when there will be a "new heaven and a new earth (Revelation 21:1 *RSVCE*)" and when "all things" will be "subjected" to his kingship (1 Corinthians 15:28 *RSVCE*).

The Israelites did not lose their sense of God's Kingship only before Samuel, and Samuel's corrupt sons, when they insisted to be like the other nations that had powerful kings. This also occurred, as the Pentateuch indicates, after the death of Joshua and at the beginning of the time of the Judges during which "there was no king in Israel" neither a human king nor acknowledgement of God as their king and the result was moral chaos as "every man did what was right in his own eyes Judges 21:25 *RSVCE*)" including horrendous acts of violence.

Beginning with the death of the second and greatest king, King David, the books of Kings narrate the second stage of the Israelites' forgetfulness of God's kingship which varied in intensity, sometimes quite minimal and other times very pronounced, especially during the reign of the morally depraved King Manasseh. 2 Kings ends with the tragic Babylonian captivity of the Kingdom of Judah in 586 B.C. Another, complementary manner of describing the bookends of 1 and 2 Kings is that it begins with King David in his final days and ends with

Zedekiah, the last of the kings of Israel.

In spiritually reflecting on these two books of Kings, we will focus on the following: Solomon, prophets, devout kings, idolatrous kings, Assyrian Exile, Babylonian Captivity, and typology.

Section Questions

1. How does God allow the Israelites to be ruled by a human king and then gradually brings the kingship back to Himself? Include in your answer the following in a specific sense: People's Rejection of Samuel as Judge, First King of Israel, Two Kingdoms, End of Kingdoms, Jesus as King

Solomon

Before sinking into vice and ever deeper moral depravity, Solomon reached heights of great acclaim for his virtue, wisdom, ability to govern with justice, and concern for people outside of his realm. Solomon's concern for non-Israelites is evident in how he dedicated the Jerusalem Temple by praying that "all peoples of the earth may know (1 Kings 8:43 *RSVCE*)" God's name and fear God.

Solomon's love for what is universal and not just what is particular to the Israelites is indicated in the beginning of his reign when he prays for wisdom, "Give your servant therefore an understanding mind to govern your people, that I may discern between good and evil; for who is able to govern this great people of yours (1 Kings 3:9 *RSVCE*)?" Upon hearing this prayer of Solomon, God is pleased because Solomon had asked for the gift of wisdom and not for a "long life, riches or the life of … enemies (1 Kings 3:11 *RSVCE*)." People from all nations travel to Solomon to learn from his wisdom (1 Kings 4:34 *RSVCE*). The universal wisdom of Solomon is capsulated in "three thousand proverbs (1 Kings 4:32 *RSVCE*)" attributed to Solomon.

[3]

Solomon and the international kingdom that foreshadows the Church[4] became so renowned that, writes Bergsma and Pitre, "for a brief moment…it appears that Israel is beginning to live out the call to be a kingdom of priests (Ex 19:5-6) and a light to the surrounding nations (Is 60:3)."[5] The First Temple that Solomon orders built to replace the moveable Tabernacle was reminiscent of the Garden of Eden and the perfection it represented. Aquinas distinguishes the spiritual significance of the movable Tabernacle from the stationary Temple built by Solomon by associating the traveling Tabernacle with

---

[3] James Tissot [Public domain], "The Wisdom of Solomon, by James Jacques Joseph Tissot (French, 1836-1902)," https://commons.wikimedia.org/wiki/File:Tissot_The_Wisdom_of_Solomon.jpg.

[4] John Bergsma and Brant Pitre, *A Catholic Introduction to the Bible, Volume I* (San Francisco: Ignatius Press, 2018), 421.

[5] Bergsma and Pitre, 390.

"the state of the present changeable life" and the Temple with the future heavenly life where all "movements of disturbance" will end.[6] Not only does Solomon's Temple represent heaven but it is also associated with the perfect time of Eden before the Fall.

An explicit association of Solomon and his Temple with the perfection of Eden is, points out Bergsma and Pitre, evident when Nathan anoints Solomon at a river identified as the Gihon (1 Kings 45).[7] This river is one of the four rivers that flowed out of Eden (Genesis 2:13). Other indicators of Solomon, his Temple, and his international kingdom as a new Eden is that like Creation which took seven days, Solomon's Temple took seven years to construct, and was, comment Bergsma and Pitre, "dedicated in the seventh month, in a festival of seven days, climaxed by a prayer of seven petitions (see I Kings 8:31, 33, 35, 37, 41, 44, 46)."[8]

Despite the association of Solomon's Temple with Eden and the many gifts Solomon received from God, including the gift of wisdom, Solomon allowed his excessive and disordered love for the goods of this world to eventually dominate him. St. Augustine cautions us from being unduly shocked by Solomon's embrace with evil: "Why marvel that Solomon fell among God's people? Did not Adam fall in paradise? Did not an angel fall from heaven and become the devil? We are thereby taught that no hope must be placed in any human being."[9]

---

[6] Thomas Aquinas, "Summa Theologiae, q. 102, art. 4, ad. 2," newadvent.org, http://www.newadvent.org/summa/2102.htm.

[7] Bergsma and Pitre, 392.

[8] Bergsma and Pitre, 392.

[9] Marco Conti, *Ancient Christian Commentary on Scripture: Old Testament V, 1-2 Kings, 1-2 Chronicles, Ezra, Nehemiah, Esther* (Downers

[10]

Solomon's weaknesses, Anderson points out, are evident right from the beginning in Solomon's willingness to kill rivals when establishing his authority as King David's successor, and after he had been officially anointed by Nathan the prophet as king.[11] As a newly

---

Grove: Intervarsity Press, 2014), 73. The following is cited: *Expositions of the Psalms* 127.1.

[10] James Tissot [Public domain], "Solomon Dedicates the Temple at Jerusalem, c. 1896-1902, by James Jacques Joseph Tissot (French, 1836-1902) or followers, gouache on board, 10 5/16 x 7 1/2 in. (26.2 x 19.2 cm), at the Jewish Museum, New York," https://commons.wikimedia.org/wiki/File:Tissot_Solomon_Dedicates_the_Temple_at_Jerusalem.jpg.

[11] William A. Anderson, *Liguori Catholic Bible Study, Historical Books II: 1 and 2 Kings, 1 and 2 Chronicles, Ezra, Nehemiah (Liguori Catholic Bible Study* (Liguori: Liguori Publications, 2013), Kindle location 409-411.

anointed king, Solomon has Adonijah, David's fourth son (2 Samuel 3:4) executed after Adonijah subtly challenges Solomon's rule by attempting to marry David's last concubine Abishag (1 Kings 2:24). Adonijah's death is followed by Solomon ordering the execution of a supporter of Adonijah, Joab, the commander of the army (1 Kings 2:31). Finally, Solomon orders the Benjamite and relative of King Saul, Shimei, to be put to death (1 Kings 46).

In time, this ruthless aspect of Solomon dominates, and Solomon severely breaks the rules God told the Israelites to follow if they choose to have a king. According to Deuteronomy, an Israelite king is not to "multiply horses for himself…multiply wives for himself…nor…multiply for himself silver and gold (Deuteronomy 17:16-17 *RSVCE*)." This legislation was to check the power of an Israelite king so that the Israelites trust primarily in God and only secondarily in an earthly king. Solomon, though, deliberately increases his power far beyond what this legislation allows, and by so doing tempts the Israelites to place excessive trust in his ability to protect them, trust that ought to be place only in God.

Solomon excessively increases his power by strengthening his military power to 12,000 horsemen, and 1,400 chariots (1 Kings 10:26), and by establishing multiple political alliances through marriages to 700 women. This intensification of power and influence is further enhanced by Solomon acquiring 300 concubines (1 Kings 11:3). The vast number of women Solomon acquired for himself, interprets Augustine, was motivated by a different kind of lust that overpowered his father, King David. The illicit lust King David had for Bathsheba passed "away like a guest," but, in Solomon, it "reigned as a king." Solomon's lust for women, power, and wealth was not as evident in his first years as king, for during his early life as a king Solomon was known for his wisdom and "spiritual love". Solomon, though, lost his spiritual love "through carnal lust."[12]

Finally, Solomon, increases his wealth by possessing 666 gold talents (1 Kings 10:14). According to Hahn, one Hebrew talent is roughly equivalent to 757 pounds.[13] This means that Solomon accumulated over 500,000 pounds of gold, clearly an excessive amount. Pitre points out that the only other time the number 666 appears in the Bible is in the Book of Revelation when referring to a number representing a diabolical beast (Revelation 13:18).[14] Mixed in with the attraction of military power, money, and pleasure that women can represent could have been the yet another motive, "to unite the nations of the world...[but] by means of his own virility, to father a thousand sons from all the nations."[15]

Solomon's desire to unite the nations was misplaced since only God is the true Father of all nations and, as God taught Abraham, God's promises will not come about through man's effort but by obedience and trust in God as the Father of all. Abram and his wife Sarah lost trust in God who had promised that they would have a child. In her impatience, Sarah told Abram to have sexual relations with her

---

[12] Augustine, "On Christian Doctrine," in *St. Augustine City of God and Christian Doctrine* (Vol. 2), ed. P. Schaff, trans. J.F. Shaw (Buffalo: Christian Literature Company, 1887), 565.

[13] Scott Hahn, *Catholic Bible Dictionary* (New York: Doubleday, 2009), 887.

[14] Brant Pitre, *The Old Testament-A Historical and Theological Journey through Jewish Scripture*, MP 3 21.

[15] Pitre, MP 3 21.

maidservant Hagar. This request, Pitre observes, was a sin since it entailed bringing about the fulfillment of God's promise by human effort.[16] Not until Abram was 99 years old and Sarah was 90 years old did God finally bless Sarah with a child, Isaac.

[17]

Solomon's efforts to bring about God's promise an everlasting Davidic kingdom (2 Samuel 7:13; cf. Exodus 4:22) fails precisely because Solomon erred by relying more and more on his own power, his own force of will, his own virility. As Solomon grew in pride, he increasingly lost sight of his creaturely status and instead began to seem himself as a necessary cause of establishing the Kingdom of God. In pride, Solomon made poor decisions based on the false belief that he was greater than he actually was. In this self-deceived state, Solomon's many non-Israelite wives led him into idolatry and even

---

[16] Pitre, MP 9.

[17] Isaak Asknaziy [Public domain], "'Vanity of vanities; all is vanity' illustrates an old and meditative King Solomon by Isaak Asknaziy," https://commons.wikimedia.org/wiki/File:Isaak_Asknaziy_02.jpeg.

into the worship of the false God Molech to whom child sacrifices were made (Leviticus 18:21).

Through Moses, God discouraged such terrible sacrifices by requiring any Israelites who sacrificed his child to Molech to be stoned to death and cut off from the chosen people (Leviticus 20:2-3). Pride, though, blinded Solomon to such an extent that he even was willing to sacrifice children to a false God with the intention of pleasing his wives and further solidifying international alliances he had through his foreign wives. Later, the very place that Solomon sacrificed children to Molech, "the valley of the son of Hinnom (Jeremiah 32:35 *RSVCE*)," became a place where trash was burned. This dump is called in the New Testament Gehenna (γέεννα, *geenna*). Gehenna, Hahn explains, is a transliteration in Greek of the Hebrew word *ge hinnom* (גֵּי הִנֹּם), which means valley of Hinnom. In the New Testament, Gehenna physically represents Hell.[18]

A related sin that Solomon committed in his zeal to bring about God's kingdom by his own power was, adds Pitre, religious syncretism.[19] By not only tolerating but also practicing the various pagan religions of his wives Solomon attempted to bring about a *Pax Solomonis* that was founded on falsehood since it was founded on Solomon usurping God's role and God's truth. In response, God tells Solomon that "I will surely tear the kingdom from you and will give it to your servant. Yet for the sake of David your father I will not do it in

---

[18] *Ignatius Catholic Study Bible, The First and Second Book of Kings, Commentary, Notes, & Study Questions, Revised Standard Version, Second Catholic Edition, with Introduction, Commentary, and Notes by Scott Hahn, and Curtis Mitch* (San Francisco: Ignatius Press, 2017), Kindle location, 5576.

[19] Pitre, MP 9.

your days, but I will tear it out of the hand of your son. However, I will not tear away all the kingdom; but I will give one tribe to your son (1 Kings 11:11-12 *RSVCE*)."

[20]

For St. Cyprian the tearing apart of Solomon's kingdom essentially distinguishes Solomon's kingdom from the Kingdom of God that Jesus embodies in himself. In identifying Jesus as the Kingdom of God, Benedict XVI writes, "Origen basing himself on a reading of Jesus' words, called Jesus the *autobasileia*, that is, the Kingdom in person. Jesus himself is the Kingdom; the Kingdom is not

[20] Charles Foster [Public domain], "Offering to Molech (illustration from the 1897 Bible Pictures and What They Teach Us by Charles Foster)," https://commons.wikimedia.org/wiki/File:Foster_Bible_Pictures_0074-1_Offering_to_Molech.jpg.

a thing; it is not a geographic dominion like worldly kingdoms. It is a person."[21] Because the Kingdom of God is Jesus and Jesus is God, unlike Solomon's kingdom, the Kingdom of God cannot be rent asunder. For this reason, Cyprian states, the seamless tunic Jesus wore at his crucifixion was not torn by the soldiers who crucified Jesus. Instead, the soldiers "cast lots for it to see whose it shall be (John 19:24 *RSVCE*)." In commenting on the symbolism of Jesus' seamless, untorn tunic, Cyprian writes, "his coat, woven throughout as a single whole, was not rent by its owners. Undivided, conjoined, coherent, it proves the unbroken harmony of our people who have put on Christ. By the type and symbol of his garment he has manifested the unity of the church."[22]

During the reign of Solomon's son, King Rehoboam, Israel's fourth king, Solomon's kingdom was torn apart by a schism between north and south. The schism took place because Rehoboam, in continuation of his father's pride, usurped God's role as the ultimate king. Rehoboam did so by ruling as a harsh, merciless totalitarian leader. The ten northern tribes reacted to Rehoboam's oppressive rule by breaking away as led by Jeroboam.

Rehoboam's sin was a continuation of his father's goal of building a visibly powerful kingdom. This entailed massive construction projects. To achieve this end, Rehoboam's father Solomon required "forced labor (1 Kings 9:15 *RSVCE*)" and taxation which enabled him to pull in one year "six hundred and sixty-six talents of gold (1 Kings

---

[21] Joseph Ratzinger, *Jesus of Nazareth: From the Baptism in the Jordan to the Transfiguration*, trans. Adrian J. Walker (New York: Doubleday, 20007), 49.

[22] Conti, 76. The following is cited: *The Unity of the Church*, 7.

10:14 *RSVCE*)." Despite being cautioned by elders to reduce his father's abuse of power, especially over the northern tribes, Rehoboam not only continued his father's lust for power but even intensified the domination by telling the northern tribes, represented by Jeroboam, that "My father made your yoke heavy, but I will add to your yoke; my father chastised you with whips, but I will chastise you with scorpions (1 Kings 12:14 *RSVCE*)." Not surprisingly, the Ephraimite Jeroboam leads the northern tribes into rebellion and the United Monarchy breaks into two.

[23]

The northern schismatic kingdom of Israel consisted of ten tribes, while the southern kingdom of Judah was made up of only two tribes: Judah and Benjamin. Soon, though the Levites, the priestly tribe, moved to the southern kingdom of Judah after "Jeroboam and his sons cast them out from serving as priests of the Lord (2 Chronicles 11:14 *RSVCE*)."

Jeroboam removed the Levites from service as priests and replaced

[23] Hans Holbein [Public domain], "The Arrogance of Rehoboam, drawing by Hans Holbein the Younger," https://commons.wikimedia.org/wiki/File:Rehoboam%27s_Insolence,_by_Hans_Holbein_the_Younger.jpg.

them with non-Levitical priests that he had appointed to offer idolatrous sacrifices on "high places" and to the two golden calves that he had made (2 Chronicles 11:15 *RSVCE*). Jeroboam had two calves of gold created for his people to worship since he feared that his people may betray him, return to Judah out of a desire to worship in the Jerusalem Temple, and kill him (1 Kings 12:27). About two hundred years after Jeroboam's idolatrous reign, during the reign of Hoshea, last king of the northern kingdom of Israel, the Assyrians in 722 B.C. conquered Israel and deported its people. The reason given is precisely for the idolatry begun by Jeroboam: "And this was so, because the sons of Israel had sinned against the Lord their God.... They built for themselves high places.... they served idols.... made for themselves molten images of two calves... they burned their sons and their daughters as offerings... (2 Kings 17:7-17 *RSVCE*)."

The Assyrian captivity of 722 B.C. began first in the lands of Galilee and Naphtali (2 Kings 155:29). As Pitre comments, Galilee and the lands of Naphtali, the place where Israel began to be deported, the location where the identity of ten tribes was lost and Israel was providentially punished for idolatry was the exact place where Jesus began his public ministry (Matthew 4:12-13). By beginning his ministry in Galilee and Naphtali, Jesus healed at its root the breakup of the Twelve Tribes Israel. He did so, explains Pitre, by gathering Twelve Apostles, who as twelve represented a new Israel with Jesus as the new Jacob-Israel, a patriarch of a new Israel that was not ethnically defined but rather open to all, evident in Jesus deliberately not calling Twelve Apostles from corresponding Twelve Tribes. The blood that binds the 12 together and the people of the new Israel is the blood of Christ. Christ's blood washes one clean at Baptism, incorporates one into a people, the Church, and is truly received at the Eucharist.[24]

[25]

Section Questions

1. How was Solomon virtuous and how did his Kingdom foreshadow the Catholic Church? Include the following in your response in a specific sense: Temple Dedication, Wisdom, Kingdom, Older Brother

---

[24] Pitre, 56.

[25] Anonymous [Public domain], "Jeroboam sets up two golden calves, from the Bible Historiale. Den Haag, MMW, 10 B 23 165r," https://commons.wikimedia.org/wiki/File:Jeroboam_sets_up_two_golden_calves.jpg.

2. How was Solomon vicious? Include the following in your response in a specific sense: Early Rivals of Solomon (Adonijah, Joab, Shimei), Horses, Wives, Solver and Gold (666), Moloch, Syncretism and Peace

3. How does God respond to Solomon's international kingdom in a way that leads to the Kingdom of Jesus Christ? Include in your answer the following in a specific sense: "Tears (1 Kings 11:11)," 722 B.C. and 586 B.C., Jesus' Seamless Tunic, Jesus' Kingdom

Prophets

Repeatedly throughout the books of Kings, God raises up prophets who call their people to repentance, warn them of consequences if they do not repent, and, from the perspective of the New Testament, prepare for Jesus Christ. These prophets are true friends, especially when they rebuke, for as Proverbs 27 teaches, "Better are the wounds of a friend, than the deceitful kisses of an enemy (Proverbs 27:6 *DRA*)."[26] Notable prophets of the books of Kings that God sends to intervene in history as true friends include Nathan, Elijah, Elisha, Ahijah the Shilonite, Isaiah, Micaiah ben Imlah, and Huldah the Prophetess.

We first encounter Nathan in the 2 Samuel where he is described as a court prophet during King David's reign. Nathan was the prophet who subtly confronted David with his adultery of Bathsheba and murder of her husband, Uriah the Hittite (2 Samuel 12:1-15). Along

---

[26] Conti, 68-69.

with other appearances, Nathan is also referred to in the first chapter of 1 Kings. In the first chapter, Nathan ensures that King David's successor will be Bathsheba's son, Solomon.

27

One of the most prominent prophets in the books of Kings appears after Solomon's United Monarchy breaks into two, Elijah. Elijah prophesied during the reign of Ahab, the seventh king of Israel since Jeroboam's schism. Ahab was ruled by his immediate desires and by his heartless wife Jezebel. When Jezebel learned that Ahab wanted a vineyard that was the precious, ancestral land of Naboth she urged her

---

[27] Anonymous [Public domain], "This common depiction of the prophet Elijah riding a flaming chariot across the sky resulted in syncretistic folklore among the Slavs incorporating pre-Christian motifs in the beliefs and rites regarding him in Slavic culture," https://commons.wikimedia.org/wiki/File:Ilia_chariot.jpg.

husband to take the land by first rewarding Naboth, and then by destroying Naboth's reputation and having Naboth stoned to death (1 Kings 21:1-16). St. Ambrose comments that although the man whose property was violently taken by king Ahab was materially poor in comparison to Naboth, this poor man, nonetheless, had spiritual riches which Ahab lacked:

> Does he not seem richer and more a king, since he had enough for himself and regulated his desires so that he wanted nothing that belonged to others? But was he not very poor whose gold was of no account, while he considered the other's vines of priceless value? Understand why he was so very poor: because riches amassed unjustly are disgorged, but the root of the righteous remains and flourishes like a palm tree.[28]

After Ahab seizes the poor man's property, Elijah, speaking on God's behalf, condemns both Ahab and Jezebel and prophecies that "dogs shall eat Jezebel (1 Kings 21:23 *RSVCE*)." In the Second Book of Kings, when Elisha, Elijah's successor, was prophesying, Jehu, the tenth king of Israel ordered Jezebel to be thrown out of a window. Jezebel splattered on the ground and was eaten by dogs (2 Kings 9:30-37).

During Ahab's reign, Elijah led a community of disciples who strove to be faithful to God. As explained by Bergsma and Pitre, "They lived in community under the guidance of the great prophets (2 Kings 6:1) and may be seen as a prototype of consecrated religious life. Some were married (2 Kings 4:1), whereas others may have been celibate like

[28] Conti, 128.

the prophets themselves: nothing is ever said of a wife or child of Elijah or Elisha."[29] St Paul in his letter to the Romans describes this small minority of faithful "Israelians"[30] as a remnant (9:27-29) and describes those who chosen by and cooperate with grace of Jesus also a remnant (11:5).

God's faithful remnant is to participate in God's gentle ways, as Bishop Barron emphasizes, who orders "all things sweetly (Wisdom 8:1 *DRA*)." This subtle, infinitely patient divine way of rectifying salvation history that is repeatedly deviated by sin was revealed to Elijah when God told Elijah, hiding from Jezebel's wrath in a cave at Mount Horeb, to "Go out and stand on the mountain before the Lord, for the Lord is about to pass by (1 Kings 19:11 *NRSV*)." Elijah obeyed and waited for God to reveal himself. Elijah witnesses powerfully violent forces of nature (strong wind, earthquake and fire) and yet God chooses not to reveal himself through any of these violent natural events as God did at other times in salvation history. Rather, God reveals himself in "a gentle blowing (1 Kings 19:12 *NAB*)" or,

---

[29] Bergsma and Pitre, 397.

[30] "All descendants of the twelve tribes, including the tribe of Judah, are 'Israelites'. The period of the divided monarchy presents terminological problems because we cannot accurately contrast 'Israelites' with 'Judeans': Judeans are Israelites. We adopt a term coined by other scholars to refer specifically to Israelites of the northern kingdom: 'Israelian'. By contrast, an Israeli is a citizen of the modern state of Israel. The term Jew (Hebrew yehudi) is first used in the books of Kings (2 Kings 16:6) and becomes common only after the exile to refer to descendants of Judah, citizens of the Judean state. It only became a primarily religious term in the pagan world of the Greco-Roman Empire and in response to the rise of Christianity." Bergsma and Pitre, 394.

according to another translation, a "still small voice (*RSVCE*)." The *RSVCE* translation is literally more accurate since the Hebrew (דַקָּה קוֹל *daqqah qol*)[31] means small voice or small sound. However, in the context of a mountain, on which Elijah is waiting for God to reveal himself through a natural phenomenon the small sound could mean a gentle breeze or blowing.

According to Ephrem the Syrian, the reason God revealed himself to Elijah in a gentle breeze was to "to instruct the prophet through various figures in order to correct excessive zeal and to lead him to imitate, according to the righteousness, the providence of the most High who regulates the judgments of his justice through the abundant mercy of his grace."[32]

Shortly after God's revelation to Elijah as a gentle breeze, Elijah chooses Elisha to be his successor. Elisha replaces Elijah after Elijah is taken up into heaven in chariot of fire drawn by horses. As Elijah leaves, his cloak falls from his shoulders. Elisha retrieves the cloak and uses it to miraculously part the Jordan river when crossing over (2 Kings 2:11-14). Similarly, comments Bede, "When our Lord ascended into heaven, he left the mysteries of the humanity he had assumed to his disciples, to the entire church in fact, so that it could be sanctified by them and warmed by the power of his love."[33]

As Elijah's successor, Elisha repeatedly reflected God's gentle loving eternal presence in the divine gentle breeze that Elijah heard on Mount Horeb. Some of the ways Elisha did so was by miraculously

---

[31] "Strong's Hebrew 6963" and "Strong's Hebrew 1827," biblehub.com.

[32] Conti, 117. The following source is cited: *On the First Book of Kings* 19:11.

[33] Conti, 145. The following source is cited: *Homilies on the Gospels*, 2:15.

providing food multiple times, including feeding a hundred men (2 Kings 4:42-44 *RSVCE*), by healing Naaman of leprosy, and even, in an act of delicate compassion, by miraculously recovering an axe head that had fallen into the water so that a servant who was using his master's axe would not be punished. In death Elisha continued to witness to God's faithful love that is greater than death. As the Second Book of Kings relates, due to a "marauding band" being seen, a funeral abruptly ended and the dead body was hastily "cast into the grave of Elisha; and as soon as the man touched the bones of Elisha, he revived, and stood on his feet (2 Kings 13:21 *RSVCE*)." This passage foreshadows the Catholic veneration of relics. The veneration of relics of saints, "when grace is more abundant, when the energy of the spirit is greater" comments John Chrysostom, also can bring about even greater miraculous events.[34]

[35]

[34] Conti, 199. The following source is cited: *Homilies on St. Ignatius and St. Babylas* 5.

[35] Sir Francis Dicksee (1853-1928) [Public domain], "Jezebel and Ahab meeting Elijah, print by Sir Francis Dicksee (1853-1928),"

Bergsma and Pitre contrast Elisha's multiple acts of mercy with Elijah's role as a prophet of justice, and judgment.[36] In the name of justice, Elijah condemned King Ahab and Queen Jezebel by warning them that they would be severely punished for being so unjust to their people. Prior to this Elijah had called together Jezebel's 450 prophets of Baal, challenged them to a contest, and then, after proving that they were false Gods, ordered them to be seized and killed (1 Kings 18:20-40). The difference between Elijah, as one who emphasizes judgment, and Elisha, as one connected more with mercy is similar, explain Bergsma and Pitre, to the relationship of John the Baptist who preached justice and judgement and whom Jesus compared with Elijah (Matthew 11:14), and Jesus, who performed multiple acts of mercy and compassion. This distinction is not to be understood to strictly since, in their own ways, adds Bergsma and Pitre, Elijah and Elisha both point to and are fulfilled in Jesus. For example, although Elijah correlates well with John the Baptist, Elijah's assumption into heaven by God's power anticipates and is fulfilled in Jesus' Ascension by His own power as God.[37]

Ahijah the Shilonite is the prophet who foretold that the northern kingdom Elijah and Elisha ministered in would one day break from Judah as a cloak is rent asunder. Ahijah prophecies this schism by tearing apart a garment into twelve pieces from which he handed ten pieces to Jeroboam while saying, "Behold, I am about to tear the kingdom from the hand of Solomon, and will give you ten tribes (1

---

https://commons.wikimedia.org/wiki/File:Jezabel-and-Ahab-Meeting-Elijah-in-Naboth-s-Vineyard.jpg.

[36] Bergsma and Pitre, 421.

[37] Bergsma and Pitre, 421-422.

Kings 11:31 *RSVCE*)." Notice that Ahijah does not tear the garment into two pieces, representing north and south, but into twelve pieces, perhaps to indicate that one day all of Israel will be rent apart and scattered among the nations, which takes place in 586 B.C. with the Babylonian exile and captivity of the southern kingdom of Judah. St. Cyprian describes this prophetic action of Ahijah as representing an essential difference between the kingdom of Israel and Jesus' kingdom of God that "subsists"[38] in the Catholic Church:

> When the twelve tribes of Israel were being rent, the prophet Ahijah rent his garment. But since Christ's people cannot be rent, his coat, woven throughout as a single whole, was not rent by its owners. Undivided, conjoined, coherent, it proves the unbroken harmony of our people who have put on Christ. By the type and symbol of his garment he has manifested the unity of the church.[39]

Later, Ahijah will once again prophecy to Jeroboam but this time when Jeroboam is king of the northern kingdom of Israel. He does so by asserting that because Jeroboam led Israel into the sin of idolatry, God will "scatter them beyond the Euphrates (1 Kings 14:15 *RSVCE*)." This takes places in 722 B.C. when the Assyrians conquer the northern kingdom, deport many and repopulate the land.

Prior to the breakup of Israel as a United Monarchy, the northern

---

[38] "Lumen Gentium, no. 8," vatican.va, http://www.vatican.va/archive/hist_councils/ii_vatican_council/documents/vat-ii_const_19641121_lumen-gentium_en.html.

[39] Conti, 76. The following is cited, *The Unity of the Church*, 7.

King Ahab consults the prophets of his land if he should jointly fight with Jehoshaphat, the king of Judah against the King of Syria (1 Kings 22:2-3). Four hundred people tell Ahab what he wanted to hear, that he would be victorious in battle. One prophet, though, a disciple of Elijah, Micaiah ben Imlah, tells the northern King Ahab that he will die in battle, Micaiah also describes a vision he experienced where an evil spirit came before God and said that "I will go forth, and will be a lying spirit" in the mouths of Ahab's prophets (1 Kings 22:22 *RSVCE*). Ahab responds to Micaiah's truthful, non-fawning prophecy by ordered him to be imprisoned until Ahab returns safely from battle. King Ahab does not return safely; instead, he is killed in battle. The true vision of Micaiah contrasts with the fictional fantasy of Ahab who in pride refused to be tempered by Micaiah's truthful foretelling of how the battle would unfold.

The temptation to be attached to fantasies of obtaining glory even if the attempt to bring the fantasy into reality by force of will may mean death, or at minimum psychological letdown due to failure, is sadly a common human experience. Sometimes, this tendency to favor fantasy over truthful visions becomes pronounced in society. On this note, St. Paul warns that "the time is coming when people will not endure sound teaching but having itching ears they will accumulate for themselves teachers to suit their own likings, and will turn away from listening to the truth and wander into myths. (2 Timothy 4:3-4 *RSVCE*)."

Benedict XVI's reflection on the relationship of prophetic visions and the future well applies to Micaiah's prophecies and to modern day prophets. These prophets are not necessarily, he writes, "to be understood as seers [of the future], but as voices who understand time from God's point of view and can therefore warn against what is destructive, - and, on the other hand, show us the right road forward."[40] Sadly, as in the case of King Ahab, a common reaction to a prophecy that reveals a future goal as a deceptive fantasy is to reject the prophet and his truthful message. Despite facing the prospect of rejection, perhaps even imprisonment as Micaiah underwent, Benedict XVI, encourages us to be open to:

> the logic of God, within apparently chance happenings. Even if this does not enable us to predict what is going to happen at this or that point, nonetheless we may develop a certain sensitivity for the dangers contained in certain things – and for the hopes that are in others. A sense of the future develops, in that I see what destroys the future – because it is contrary to the inner logic of the road – and what, on the other hand, leads onward – because it opens the positive doors and corresponds to the inner design of the whole. To that extent the ability to diagnose the future can develop.[41]

King Hezekiah was the southern king of Judah who witnessed the end of the northern Kingdom of Israel in 722 B.C. due to the repeated sins of idolatry promoted by kings like Ahab. The great southern kingdom prophet Isaiah miraculously healed King Hezekiah from a life-threatening illness, enabling him to live fifteen years more (2 Kings 20:6). Isaiah also assured Hezekiah that the southern kingdom would

---

[40] Benedict XVI, *Day by Day with Pope Benedict XVI*, ed. Peter John Cameron (San Francisco: Ignatius Press, 2006), 42.

[41] Benedict XVI, *Day by Day with Pope Benedict XVI*, 42.

not be conquered by the Assyrians who defeated the Kingdom of Israel and deported its people. However, Isaiah also prophecies that one day the Southern Kingdom of Judah will experience a similar defeat and deportation.

[42]

"Behold the days are coming," prophecies Isaiah to King Hezekiah thirteenth king of Judah, "when all that is in your house, and that which your fathers have stored up till this day, shall be carried to Babylon; nothing shall be left, says the Lord (2 Kings 20:17 *RSVCE*)." Almost 140 years later, in 586 B.C. the Kingdom of Judah is similarly conquered by an empire, the Babylonian Empire, and deported. Unlike, Israel, though, the Jewish people who were deported to Babylon return home when the Persian King Cyrus the Great issues an

---

[42] Gerard Hoet (1648-1733) [Public domain], "Gerard Hoet, Ahijah's prophecy to Jeroboam, 1728," https://commons.wikimedia.org/wiki/File: Ahijahs_and_Jeroboam.jpg.

edict that allows the Jewish people to return their homeland (2 Chronicles 36:22-23).

[43]

The prophecy that the Kingdom of Judah would also be collectively punished was repeated a few kings later, when King Josiah was ruling Judah. This time the prophecy came through a woman prophetess, Huldah. Huldah warns King Josiah that since the people of Judah have repeatedly worshipped false Gods, the land and its people will "become a desolation and curse (2 Kings 22:19 *RSVCE*)."

Section Questions

1. Name the prophet who denounced David's sin of adultery and murder.

2. How do Elijah and Elisha correlate to John the Baptist and Jesus and specifically why? Include in your answer the

---

[43] James Tissot [Public domain], "James Tissot, The Flight of the Prisoners – the fall of Jerusalem, 586 BCE," https://commons.wikimedia.org/wiki/File:Tissot_The_Flight_of_the_Prisoners.jpg.

following: Judgment, Mercy, Jezebel's Prophets, Elisha's Miracles

Devout Kings

King Josiah responded to Huldah's prophecy by "deposing the idolatrous priests whom the kings of Judah had ordained (2 Kings 23:5 *RSVCE*)." These priests had led the people of Judah in false worship "to Ba'al, to the sun, and the moon, and the constellations, and all the host of the heavens (2 Kings 23:5 *RSVCE*)." Josiah was so zealous in bringing his people back to true worship that 2 Kings praises him with, "Before him there was no king like him, who turned to the Lord with all his heart…nor did any like him arise after him (2 Kings 23:25 *RSVCE*)." Another, southern king known for his reform is King Hezekiah, who preceded Manasseh, Amon, and Josiah.

Like King Josiah, Hezekiah "did what was right in the eyes of the Lord (2 Kings 18:3 *RSVCE*)." This phrase is also used to describe to described King Jehoshaphat (1 Kings 22:43) and to King Jotham (2 Kings 15:34), but it applies more properly to Hezekiah because unlike both King Jehoshaphat and King Jotham, who tolerated the idolatry of their people, Hezekiah refused to tolerate idolatry and set about eradicating idolatrous practices in his kingdom. His people had become so idolatrous that they even were worshipping the bronze serpent that God had told Moses to make for the Israelites to look at so as to be healed from bites by "fiery serpents (Numbers 21:6 *RSVCE*)." To prevent his people from worshipping this bronze serpent, Hezekiah broke it into pieces (2 Kings 18:4). As is evident, Hezekiah was not simply content to be righteous himself while ignoring the unrighteousness of his people.

[44]

Sadly, Hezekiah was succeeded by a very wicked son, Manasseh, who promoted idolatry like the majority of the kings of Judah and Israel.

Section Questions

1. Why are King Josiah and King Hezekiah praised in the books of Kings? Include in your answer the following: Bronze Serpent, Idolatry

[44] The story of the Bible from Genesis to Revelation [Public domain], "Josiah hearing the book of the law (1873)," https://commons.wikimedia.org/wiki/File:Josiah_hearing_the_book_of_the_law.jpg.

Idolatrous Kings

Manasseh became king of Judah at only twelve years old when he began co-reigning with his father Hezekiah. In all, Manasseh reigned for fifty-five years (2 Kings 21:1).[45] He was the first king of Judah after the Assyrian exile of the northern kingdom of Israel. Instead of avoiding idolatry out of holy fear that the Judah also could undergo an exile as Israel did, Manasseh did precisely the opposite and reversed all the good reforms instituted by his father Hezekiah. In rebuilding idolatrous alters and promoting idolatrous practices Manasseh even engaged in child sacrifice by burning his own "son as an offering (2 Kings 21:6 *RSVCE*)."

The shedding of his son's innocent blood is but one instance of Manasseh's ruthlessness. As 2 Kings states, "Manasseh shed very much innocent blood, till he had filled Jerusalem from one end to another (2 Kings 21:16 *RSVCE*)." His propensity for violence, love of death, and desire to dominate by killing well places him within the civilization of death, named by St. Augustine as the City of Man, represented by Cain's city.

The book of Chronicles adds that near the end of his life Manasseh was taken captive by Assyrian army commanders who brought him to Babylon in chains. This providential captivity provided Manasseh with an almost unavoidable opportunity to face his ugliness, turn to the Lord for mercy and repent, which he did. God then subtly arranged history for Manasseh to return to Jerusalem. Upon returning to Jerusalem, Manasseh attempted to undo the tremendous harm he had done to his land and people by removing false idols and restoring true

[45] *Ignatius Catholic Study Bible,* Kindle location, 5450.

worship of God (2 Chronicles 33:10-17).

[46]

Manasseh's repentance and conversion are some of the many ways where God offers salvific hope to all, even to the most hardened of sinners. As John Chrysostom explains:

> For so Manasseh had perpetrated innumerable pollutions, having both stretched out his hands against the saints, and brought abominations into the temple, and filled the city with murders and wrought many other things beyond excuse; yet nevertheless after so long and so great wickedness, he washed

[46] The Providence Lithograph Company [Public domain], "Manasseh's repentance; as in 2 Chronicles 33:1-13 (illustration from a Bible card published in 1904 by the Providence Lithograph Company)," https://commons.wikimedia.org/wiki/File:Manasseh%27s_Sin_and_Repentance_(Bible_Card).jpg.

> away from himself all these things. How and in what matter? By repentance and self-examination. For there is no sin that does not yield and give way to the power of repentance, or rather to the grace of Christ. Since if we would but only change, we have him to assist us. And if you are desirous to become good, there is not to hinder us; or rather there is one to hinder us, the devil, yet he has no power, so long as you choose what is best and so attract God to your aid.[47]

Despite Manasseh's repentance and despite the consistent good rule of King Josiah, "Still the Lord did not turn from the fierceness of his great wrath, by which his anger was kindled against Judah, because of all the provocations with which Manasseh had provoked him (2 Kings 23:26 *RSVCE*)." This can be understood as the practices of idolatry, destruction and violence that Manasseh had practiced and promoted had become so entrenched in Judah that only by an extraordinary intervention by God could these be uprooted. Instead, God, in his infinitely patient wisdom, allowed the self-destructive penalties of these evil habits and acts to be experienced by Judah. Thus, the southern Kingdom of Judah in 586 B.C. underwent its own exile and banishment.

Even though the 2 Kings ends with the Babylonian exile of the Kingdom of Judah, it does so on a note of hope by describing King Jehoiachin being freed from imprisonment in Babylon by Evil-Merodach and given "a seat above the seats of the kings who were with him in Babylon (2 Kings 25:29 *RSVCE*)." Later, in the same century,

[47] Conti, 227. The following source is cited: *Homilies on the Gospel of Matthew*, 22:6.

after King Cyrus defeated the Babylonians, Cyrus issued a decree allowing the Jewish people to return to their homeland and rebuild.[48] The time of the Babylonian Captivity that the Jewish people were released from by King Cyrus was a blessing in disguise for in Babylon the Jewish people strengthened their relationship with God by retaining their worship of God even though they were outside of the Promised Land they associated with God. This fidelity led to the development of, Miller explains, "Judaism" that is distinct from political/national affiliation by worshipping in the small, multiple Bible centered synagogue worship not dependent on the one fixed place of Jerusalem Temple worship.[49] According to Miller this approach to worship was "unheard of". He explains:

> In the ancient world, it was unheard of that a people would leave the land belonging to their god and yet continue to serve that god. Most people just figured out who the god of their new home was and became adherents of that deity. But the Judeans exiled to Babylon—who now became Babylonian citizens—

---

[48] Bergsma and Pitre, 448.

[49] Robert D. Miller II, *Understanding the Old Testament* (Chantilly: The Teaching Company, 2019), 226. "A place where Jews gather to hear the scriptures, pray, and sing is called a synagogue. It is in the Babylonian exile that the word synagogue first appears, mentioned in the book of Ezekiel. Unfortunately, no synagogues have ever been found in ancient Iraq from this period, so we can't be certain. Although many of the festivals of the Jewish calendar would become impossible without the Temple, it was certainly possible to keep the sabbath. Kosher diet laws could be maintained, circumcision preserved. All of these things, in fact, became more important in exile, so the community could distinguish itself from its neighbors."

> still practiced the religion of Judah. So, they really formed what we can now call a religion. The word "religion" really didn't make any sense until this time. Faith was part of citizenship. But for the Jews in Babylon, religious faith was now distinct from social nationality.[50]

While in exile the Jewish people retained, though, a political hope for a reunion of their religion with their national home. This political hope that comes true with King Cyrus's decree is gradually transformed as it, writes Benedict XVI, "points less and less to an earthly and political power."[51] This transformation and purification of hope, is especially evident in Jesus who even expresses, comments Benedict XVI, caution with "the title of messiah" due to its political connotations. "This becomes apparent, for example" writes Benedict XVI:

> in Jesus' remark concerning the messiah as son of David according to Psalm 110. Jesus recalls that the scribes portray the messiah as the son of David. In the Psalm, however, the messiah does not appear as David's son, but as his Lord (Mk 12:35f). Even when, in the confessional formula that was developing among the apostles, the title Christ-Messiah is applied to Jesus, he immediately supplements and corrects the ideas concealed in this title with a catechesis on the suffering

---

[50] Miller, 227.

[51] Benedict XVI, "Grace and Vocation Without Remorse: Comments on the Treatise De Iudaeis," *Communio* 45 (Spring 2018), 173.

of the savior (see Mk 8:27–33; Mt 16:13–23).[52]

The hope present in the Old Testament is grounded in trust that God is faithful to his promises, including to the promise made to King David that "your house and your kingdom shall be made sure for ever before me; your throne shall be established for ever (2 Samuel 7:16 *RSVCE*)." Since God is faithful to his word, the *Catechism of the Catholic Church* teaches that "the Old Covenant has never been revoked (121)."[53] The never-revoked Davidic Covenant, though, has undergone a number of transformations as God respects the freedom of those He elects for salvation to reject His covenantal relationship.[54] The respect God has for human freedom entails allowing His chosen to undergo "cursed" times so that experiencing the false promises of sin that ultimately ends in misery they will "in their distress" turn back "to the Lord (2 Chronicles 15:4 *RSVCE*)." Faithful to His covenantal relationship that develops in time in response to the free choices that God's human partners make, God sends his only-begotten Son Jesus, of the House of David (Matthew 1:1-17), to continue the Kingdom of David in the Catholic Church.[55]

---

[52] Benedict XVI, "Grace and Vocation Without Remorse," 173-174.

[53] "Catechism of the Catholic Church, no. 121," ccc.usccb.org, http://ccc.usccb.org/flipbooks/catechism/files/assets/basic-html/page-34.html.

[54] Benedict XVI, "Grace and Vocation Without Remorse," 184.

[55] *Ignatius Catholic Study Bible, The First and Second Book of Kings, Commentary, Notes, & Study Questions, Revised Standard Version, Second Catholic Edition, with Introduction, Commentary, and Notes by Scott Hahn, and Curtis Mitch* (San Francisco: Ignatius Press, 2017), Kindle location 3271.

Section Questions

1. Who was King Manasseh's father and how was King Manasseh very different from his father. Finally, according to the second book of Chronicles, near then end of his life how did King Manasseh change? Include in your answer the following: Idolatry, Captivity.

Typology

The, at times, pronounced political hope of Israel can be seen as a type of the New Testament spiritual hope in heaven that is here but not yet in its fullness, for Jesus says both that "the kingdom of God is in your midst (Luke 17:21 *RSVCE*) and "My kingship is not of this world (John 18:36 *RSVCE*)." The fullness of the kingdom of God will only occur when all of created reality is transformed fully by God into a new heaven and new earth (Revelation 21:1 *RSVCE*), where "Christ is all and in all (Colossians 3:11 *RSVCE*)."

Mary is the human person who anticipates this perfected time when heaven and earth will kiss and all earthly realities will be taken up by heavenly reality and transformed perfectly "without spot or wrinkle (Ephesians 5:27 *RSVCE*)." Mary "is," John Paul II teaches, "a type of the Church, not as an imperfect prefiguration, but as the spiritual fullness."[56]

Mary is prefigured in the books of Kings, principally in Solomon's

---

[56] John Paul II, "Mary is Outstanding Figure of Church, August 1997," ewtn.com, https://www.ewtn.com/library/PAPALDOC/JP2BVM58.HTM, no. 3.

mother, Bathsheba, who was a Queen Mother. As explained by Hahn, because powerful men in West Asia often had many wives, it was difficult to choose one of the women to be the queen since this choice could lead to unwanted conflicts. This was even more the case when kings married various women for political reasons. To eliminate this source of conflict, a custom arose that recognized the mother of the king as queen.

[57]

An important example of a queen mother (*gebirah*, גְּבִירָה) in the books of Kings is Bathsheba, mother of Solomon. As Queen Mother she was entitled to a sit on a throne to the right of her son. In that position she offered advice to her son and interceded for people to her powerful son (1 Kings 2:13-19; Psalm 45:9; Proverbs 31). As the fulfillment of Bathsheba and all Queen Mothers, Mary intercedes for all people to her son our heavenly king, who in his infinite patient mercy listens to his queen mother. New Testament indications of

[57] Rokitno Sanctuary [Public domain], "Crowned Madonna, Rokitno, Poland, 1671," https://commons.wikimedia.org/wiki/File:Matka-Boza_Rokitno.jpg.

Mary's status as queen mother to Jesus are, points out Pitre, Mary's older cousin Elizabeth greeting her as "the mother of my Lord (Luke 1:43 *RSVCE*)," the Marian woman figure in Revelation chapter twelve who is crowned with twelve stars, representing the twelve tribes of Israel and the new Israel of the Twelve Apostles. The distinction between Mary as Queen and Jesus as King was clearly maintained in early Catholic veneration of Mary, explains Pitre, by only offering sacrifices to God in adoration and never to Mary, and if this occurred such idolatrous practice was condemned.[58]

To understand how Jesus as King relates to the time of the kings, especially to King David and King Solomon, it is necessary to know with greater precision the meaning of covenant. As well explained by Benedict XVI, when using the term covenant, it is important to acknowledge that in Romans "Paul does not speak of the 'covenant' but of 'covenants.'" Benedict XVI further adds that, "For the Old Testament, 'covenant' is a dynamic reality that is concretized in an unfolding series of covenants."[59] The various forms of implicit and explicit covenants include God's covenants with creation, with Adam, with Noah, with Abraham, with Moses, with Jacob/Israel, and with David. None of these covenants are exact duplicates of preceding covenants. Rather, there is both continuity and change, or more precisely, development.

For example, as Bergsma and Pitre show, the Mosaic and the

---

[58] *Ignatius Catholic Study Bible,* Kindle location 1749-1788; Brant Pitre, *Jesus and the Jewish Roots of Mary: Unveiling the Mother of the Messiah* (New York: Crown Publishing Group, 2018), Kindle locations 1,197, 1239, 1396-1398

[59] Benedict XVI, "Grace and Vocation Without Remorse," 181.

Davidic covenant are in continuity with one another in a way that is "complementary rather than contradictory"[60] even though there are many important differences including the location where the two covenants were made (Sinai vs. Zion), the dominant type of sacrifice (Burnt Offering vs. Thanksgiving Offering), type of instruction (Law vs. Wisdom), and type of nation (national vs. international).[61]

The explanation for these differences are clearly seen when both the Mosaic covenant and the Davidic covenant are viewed in relationship to Jesus who fulfills the Old Testament covenants by being present with us as Immanuel in this everchanging world, represented, comments Aquinas, by the movable Tabernacle, and as being our final destiny, represented by the stability of Solomon's Temple.[62] Jesus also fulfills both covenants by offering himself totally, like the Mosaic burnt offerings, on the cross and by giving us the Eucharist by which we thank God for having given us his only-begotten Son. Christ also is both transcendent law, by being the eternally spoken word of the Father, and is immanent practical wisdom by being born in time. Finally, Jesus's Kingdom is both a national kingdom and an international kingdom. Jesus' establishment of the Twelve Apostles, and, consequently a college of bishops and

---

[60] Bergsma and Pitre, 416.

[61] Bergsma and Pitre, 416.

[62] Thomas Aquinas, "Summa Theologiae, I-II, Q. 102. Art. 4," newadvent.org, http://www.newadvent.org/summa/2102.htm#article4. "The figurative reason may be assigned to the fact that they signify a twofold state. For the tabernacle, which was changeable, signifies the state of the present changeable life: whereas the temple, which was fixed and stable, signifies the state of future life which is altogether unchangeable."

their associated local churches represents the national dimension of the Church, in continuity with the Mosaic nation, and is international, due to the Pope, successor of Peter and Vicar of Christ, who, through Christ, integrates all national expressions of Catholicism into an international Church, in whom all are invited to salvation.

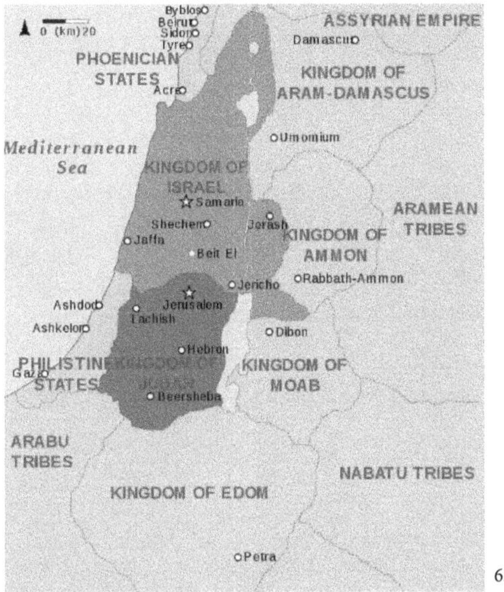

63

Section Questions

1. How does Solomon's mother Bathsheba prefigure Mary? Include in your answer the following: Queen Mother, Throne, Intercession

[63] Oldtidens_Israel_&_Judea.svg: FinnWikiNoderivative work: Richardprins [CC BY-SA 3.0 (https://creativecommons.org/licenses/by-sa/3.0)], "Map of the region in the 9th century BCE," https://commons.wikimedia.org/wiki/File:Kingdoms_of_Israel_and_Judah_map_830.svg.

2. Compare the Mosaic Covenant with the Davidic Covenant. Then, comment on how the Catholic Church fulfills both the uniqueness of the Mosaic Covenant and the uniqueness of the Davidic Covenant. Include the following in your response: Sinai, Burnt Offering, Law, Nation, Local

1 Chronicles and 2 Chronicles

Introduction

The Greek title Chronicles is based on the word *chronos* (χρόνος) which means time, in the sense of measurable motion through space. This concept of time by emphasizing time quantifiably, as a "succession of moments"[1] is distinct from another Greek term for time, *kairos* (καιρός). *Kairos* defines time qualitatively, and for this reason is based on the Greek word *kara* (κάρα or κάρη) meaning head, since it can be used to indicate a time in which something finds its fulfillment, it's head, so to speak. Kairos is used in a number of places in the New Testament, for example in Mark's gospel when time is described as "fulfilled" since Jesus has come, the term *kairos* is used and not *chronos*, "Jesus came into Galilee, preaching the gospel of God, and saying, 'The time [*kairos*] is fulfilled, and the Kingdom of God is at hand (Mark 1:14-15 *RSVCE*)'."[2]

From a Catholic perspective the book of Chronicles is suitably named since it describes a sequence of events that find their head, their fulfilment, their *kairos* in the New Testament, who is Jesus. A distinction similar to how *chronos* differs from *kairos* is made in the New Testament between *bios* (βίος) and *zoe* (ζωή). Bios, which the

---

[1] "5550. chronos," biblehub.com, https://biblehub.com/greek/5550.htm.

[2] "5550. chronos," biblehub.com, https://biblehub.com/greek/5550.htm; "2540. kairos," biblehub.com, https://www.biblehub.com/greek/2540.htm.

English word biology and biography is based on, refers to life, physically and materially understood.[3] For example, Luke uses the term *bios*, when depicting Jesus referring in the Parable of the Sower to people who hear the word but due to the "cares and riches and pleasures of life (*bios*), … their fruit does not mature (Luke 8:14 *RSVCE*)." In contrast *zoe* is used in the New Testament when referring to eternal, everlasting, spiritual life that man in his physicality is called to. When in Matthew's gospel the Rich Young Man asks Jesus "Teacher who good deed must I do, to have eternal life (Matthew 19:16 *RSVCE*)?" the term *zoen* (ζωὴν) is used.

With respect to the New Testament, the book of Chronicles emphasizes the physical, created life that is in chronological time, while the New Testament brings out more the uncreated, eternal life (*zoe*) that human beings are called in Jesus to participate in. Since by having bodies, human beings are not angels what is the relationship between the chronological, created life emphasized in Chronicles with the eternal, uncreated life repeatedly highlighted by the New Testament? Benedict XVI responds to this question by referring to an Augustinian concept, Benedict XVI terms "memory-time".

As Benedict explains, when humans die and, God willing, participate in a definitive manner in God's eternal life their relationship to the physical, biological, chronological world is not completely severed. Instead, the memory of time as chronological, and the life as physical carries over into eternal life and is transformed. As Benedict phrases this, "When we die, we step beyond history. In a preliminary fashion, history is concluded-for me. But this does not mean that we lose our relation to history: the network of human

[3] "979. bios," biblehub.com, https://biblehub.com/greek/979.htm.

relationality belongs to human nature itself."[4] The history described in Chronicles, which includes a good number events that the two books of Kings passes over, is relevant to the New Testament and the New Testament's emphasis on the eternal and spiritual since God did not come to destroy that which he created but rather to transform, perfect and beautify all of creation as the miraculously burning bush that Moses saw was not consumed by the divine fire but rather perfectly reordered, and glorified by it (Exodus 3:2).

Additions to Books of Kings

The standard English title for the books of Chronicles originates from Saint Jerome, explains Hahn, who, "called them a *chronicon totius divinae historiae*, or 'chronicle of the entire divine history'." Prior to Jerome, the Septuagint Greek translation of the Old Testament named these books *Paraleipomena*, which means in Greek "Things Omitted". According to this more ancient title, the books contain details of salvation history that were passed over and not mentioned in previous books, especially the preceding books of Kings and Samuel.[5] A number of notable examples are the special importance the Kingdom of Judah is given, accounts of King David's liturgical reforms, and King Manasseh's surprising conversion to God from near total depravity.

---

[4] Joseph Ratzinger, *Eschatology: Death and Eternal Life, Second Edition*, trans. Michael Waldstein (Washington: The Catholic University of America Press, 1988), 184-185.

[5] Scott Hahn, *Catholic Bible Dictionary* (New York: Doubleday, 2009), 146.

Section Questions

1. What does the Greek word *Chronos* mean that forms the basis of the word Chronicles? What does the word *Kairos* mean in Greek and how does it differ from *Chronos*?

2. The Greek Septuagint title for Chronicles is *Paraleipomena*, meaning "Things Omitted". Why specifically is this a suitable title for Chronicles?

Judah's Importance

Unlike the books of Kings, Chronicles almost exclusively focuses on the southern Kingdom of Judah while only occasionally referring to the northern Kingdom of Israel. This focus allows Chronicles to bring out details concerning the Kingdom of Judah that are not present in the books of Kings, which focus on both kingdoms.

As Bergsma and Pitre explain, Chronicles bring out the strength of kingdom of Judah by noting their military victories. In addition, Chronicles adds to the liturgical reforms of King Josiah by describing reforms other Judean kings had implemented including Manasseh, after his conversion.[6]

---

[6] John Bergsma and Brant Pitre, *A Catholic Introduction to the Bible, Volume I* (San Francisco: Ignatius Press, 2018), 437. The kings listed by Bergsma and Pitre whose military victories are highlighted by Chronicles are "Abijam, Asa, Jehoshaphat, Amaziah, Uzziah, Hezekiah," and the kings who instituted liturgical reforms before Josiah are, "Asa, Jehoshaphat, Joash, Hezekiah, Manasseh".

In the process of concentrating on the southern kingdom of Judah and bringing out its strengths, Chronicles does not completely ignore the northern kingdom of Israel, carefully add Bergsma and Pitre. One notable example is that Chronicles refers to people from the northern Kingdom of Israel immigrating to the Kingdom of Judah. 2 Chronicles 11:14-17 describes Levites leaving Israel and immigrating to Judah in protest of King Jeroboam appointing his own priesthood. In 2 Chronicles 15:9-15 the southern King of Judah, Asa, third king of the separated Kingdom of Judah, is described as attracting immigrants from the northern Kingdom of Israel who had heard of King Asa's liturgical reforms. These immigrants included members from the Tribes of "Ephraim, Manasseh and Simeon (2 Chronicles 15:9 *RSVCE*)."[7] Along with the Levites, members from these three tribes settled with the two southern tribes of Judah and Benjamin.

The reason Chronicles repeatedly stresses that the representatives from many tribes settled in the southern Kingdom of Judah is to teach that, explain Bergsma and Pitre, "the people of Judah have assimilated persons from all the tribes and thus are the legitimate successor of the twelve tribes of Israel, all twelve of whom were party to the covenant with the Lord and, therefore, must be part of the anticipated restoration."[8] The full restoration of all the tribes begins to take place with the coming of Jesus. As mentioned previously, following his heavenly Father's will, Jesus, a descendant of King David (Matthew 1; Romans 1:3) begins his public ministry in northern Israel, in the lands of Galilee and Naphtali (Matthew 4:12-13), the site where in 722 B.C.

---

[7] 1 Kings 12:21-23; Deuteronomy 10:9; Numbers 18:24; 1 Chronicles 4:42.

[8] Bergsma and Pitre, 440.

the Assyrian Empire began to deport the first people of the ten tribes that lost their corporate identity.

Section Questions

1. Which Kingdom does Chronicles focus on, but not exclusively, southern or northern and why, according to Bergsma and Pitre, is it emphasized in Chronicles that the Southern Kingdom has representatives from many tribes?

King David

The Church relates King David to Jesus by adding an essential verse from David's public praise of God given near the end of David's life to the Our Father prayer.[9] The verse David prayed is, "Yours, O Lord, is the greatness, and the power, and the glory, and the victory, and the majesty (1 Chronicles 29:11 *RSVCE*)." Similarly, Our Father's doxology when prayed at Mass is, "For the kingdom, the power, and the glory are yours, now and forever." According to the *Catechism of the Catholic Church*, kingship, power, and glory affirmed in this doxology are properly attributed to Christ and not to, "The ruler of this world [who] has mendaciously attributed to himself the three titles of kingship, power, and glory (*CCC* 2855)."[10]

[9] Bergsma and Pitre, 444.

[10] "Catechism of the Catholic Church," no. 2855, vatican.va, http://www.vatican.va/archive/ccc_css/archive/catechism/p4s2a4.htm.

[11]

Every time Catholics participate in a Mass we are reminded of a kind of kingship, power, and glory that is markedly different than how these three realities are typically displayed in the world, a world where rulers use power and glory as a way to dominate, "lord it over" those

[11] "Statue of King David by Nicolas Cordier in the Borghese Chapel of the Basilica di Santa Maria Maggiore," Jastrow [Public domain], https://commons.wikimedia.org/wiki/File:David_SM_Maggiore.jpg.

who they rule over. Jesus teaches, "You know that the rulers of the Gentiles lord it over the. It shall not be so among you; but whoever would be great among you must be your servant, and whoever would be first among you must be your slave; even as the Son of man came not to be served but to serve, and to give his life as a ransom for many (Matthew 20:25-28 *RSVCE*)."

Despite King David never having worshipped other gods, and having established, as Hahn, Bergsma and Pitre term it, a "liturgical empire" [12] centered on right worship of God, David nonetheless failed repeatedly to manifest kingship, power, and glory according to the how God wants these three realities to be lived out. David's lording it over his subjects by misusing power is especially evident in his adultery with Bathsheba and murder of her husband Uriah the Hittite. This grave abuse of power, however, is followed by David humbling himself before God as Psalm 51 well testifies to, "Have mercy on me, O God, ... Wash me thoroughly from my iniquity and cleanse me from my sin! (Psalm 51:1-2 *RSVCE*)."

Due to David's shedding Uriah the Hittite blood and shedding much more blood in wars, God commands David "not to build a house to my name 1 Chronicles (1 Chronicles 22:8 *RSVCE*)." This would be accomplished by Solomon, who also fell far short from living out kingship, power and glory in the humble manner God desires. Only in Jesus whose earthly crown was a crown of thorns, whose throne was the cross, and who never shed blood but rather shed his own blood and by so doing revealed his heavenly Father's will of transforming the terrible death of Jesus into a glorious act by the Resurrection of Jesus from the dead. In this way, Jesus was the final Davidic King who fulfills

[12] Bergsma and Pitre, 440.

the divine promise that "the Lord would not destroy Judah, for the sake of David his servant, since he promised to give a lamp to him and to his sons forever (2 Kings 8:19 *RSVCE*)."

David prepared for Jesus coming in yet another way, by actions that anticipate and point to the coming of Jesus in the womb of Mary. As Bergsma and Pitre explain, the Church's liturgy on the Feast of the Assumption of Mary teaches this typology. The Assumption Mass's first reading (1 Chronicles 15:3-4,15-16; 16:1-2) describes David accompanying the Ark, bearing the Ten Commandments, to Jerusalem. Within the context of the liturgy, the ark is a sign of Mary who bore in her womb Jesus. Jesus is the New Law who gives grace that enables us to not only to live in accordance with the Old Law but also to surpass it. The relationship with Jesus, in the Holy Spirit, directed to the Heavenly Father is grace because only through Jesus are we capable of participating in divine nature (2 Peter 1:4) and, consequently, capable of living in accordance with truth that sets us free (John 8:32). By accompanying the Ark to Jerusalem, David foreshadows Jesus who assumed his Blessed Mother into heaven, the heavenly Jerusalem, where the saints and angels relate to one another through Jesus in perfect, joyful, harmony.[13]

Section Questions

1. What Liturgical Feast Day has as its first reading the First Book of Chronicles account of David accompanying the Ark with joy to Jerusalem and why? Include in your response the following: Mary, New Law, Ten Commandments, Heaven

---

[13] Bergsma and Pitre, 444.

King Manasseh's Conversion

The account of King Manasseh's conversion provides a hope within Chronicles that is not as evident in the 1 and 2 Kings. Before his conversion, King Manasseh had gained the reputation of being one of the most wicked kings of history, and not only of Israelite history, as 2 Kings states, "Manasseh seduced them [his people] to do more evil than the nations had done whom the Lord destroyed before the sons of Israel (2 Kings 21:9 *RSVCE*)."

Manasseh's repentance, turning away from his evil ways, and instituting kingdom wide liturgical reform (2 Chronicles 33:15-16) offers hope to all, even the most hardened of sinners, that God is patiently waiting to mercifully receive us back into right relationship with him no matter how much one has sinned. The condition, though, is a contrite heart, humble acknowledgement of our sinfulness, and cooperation in God's plan of salvation.

Salvation history is the context of Manasseh's conversion that is explicitly detailed by 1 Chronicles. The book begins with Adam and then traces God's providential plans to Abraham, and then from Abraham to and after the Babylonian captivity of Judah (1 Chronicles 9:1 ff.). "[B]y tracing the genealogies from creation to the present, the Chronicler gives the important message," explain Bergsma and Pitre, "to his readers that the contemporary generation, however troubled it may be, is still part of God's plan of salvation."[14] Manasseh's conversion is a testimony to God's persistence presence of grace ever beckoning one to amend one's errant ways. As Cardinal Newman describes God's salvific will in history, "Such is God's will, gathering

[14] Bergsma and Pitre, 434.

in His elect, first one and then another, by little and little, in the intervals of sunshine between storm and storm, or snatching them from the surge of evil, even when the waters rage most furiously."[15]

Section Questions

1. What is the name of the King who is described in the two books of Kings for his great evil is recorded in the Second Book of Chronicles as converting?

[15] John Henry Newman, *The Via Media of the Anglican Church, Vol. I* (London: Basil Montagu Pickering, 1877), 355.

Ezra and Nehemiah

Introduction

The book of Ezra and the book of Nehemiah focus on two people, the priest Ezra and the layman Nehemiah. Ezra and Nehemiah lead the Jewish people back to their homeland and back to observing the Mosaic law. This return is made possible by the Persian King Cyrus (c. 600-530 B.C.) who issues a proclamation addressed to the Jewish people "to go up to Jerusalem, which is in Judah, and rebuild the house of the Lord (1 Ezra 1:3 *RSVCE*)." According to Ezra, Cyrus's proclamation was made in the first year of the king's reign. Cyrus's reign began after he successfully defeated the Babylonians who had deported the people of Judah by order of King Nebuchadnezzar, King of Babylon.

Zerubbabel "the son of Shealtiel (Ezra 3:2 *RSVCE*)" is the main leader of the exiles returning to their homeland. Upon returning to Jerusalem, Zerubbabel organized his people to rebuild the Temple (Ezra 3:8). The following chapter describes the Samaritans, "people of the land (Ezra 4:4 *RSVCE*),"[1] as offering to help Zerubbabel to rebuild

---

[1] The Samaritans are called after the fourth capital of the Northern Kingdom of Israel (1 Kings 16:24). The other capital cities were Shechem (Joshua 21:20-21), Penuel (1 Kings 12:25), and Tirzah (1 Kings 15:33). During the Assyrian conquest in 722 B.C. of the Northern Kingdom, the Assyrians settled non-Israelites in Samaria who intermarried with the native

the Temple, but he rejects their offer and they in turn retaliate by sending a letter to the Persian King Artaxerxes (likely Artaxerxes I 465-424 B.C.),[2] warning the king that if he allows the Jewish people to rebuild Jerusalem's Temple, city and walls, they will eventually stop paying taxes to Persia (Ezra 4:11, 13). Heeding this warning, the King ends the restoration of the temple, city and walls.

God then inspires the prophets Haggai and Zechariah (Ezra 5:1 *RSVCE*) to tell the people to start rebuilding the Temple (Ezra 5:1). Heeding the prophets, Zerubbabel once again leads his people in rebuilding the Temple even without official permission from the current king Darius. Eventually, by appealing to a decree of King Cyrus, Zerubbabel receives permission from King Darius to rebuild the Temple and city. Supported by King Darius, Zerubbabel ensures that the Temple is rebuilt, dedicated and Passover is celebrated (Ezra 6).

Section Questions

1. Where did the Edict of King Cyrus (c. 600-530 B.C.) allow the Jewish people to go?

Ezra

Years later, the Persian King Artaxerxes writes a letter to the priest

---

people. A religion developed then developed in Samaria that was partly Israelite and partly pagan (2 Kings 17: 24-41).

[2] John Bergsma and Brant Pitre, *A Catholic Introduction to the Bible, Volume I* (San Francisco: Ignatius Press, 2018), 455.

Ezra (Ezra 7:12 *RSVCE*). The letter grants permission to Ezra and "any of the sons of Israel or their priests or Levites (Ezra 7:13 *RSVCE*)" to return to Jerusalem and offer proper worship to God "lest His wrath be against the realm of the king and his sons (Ezra 7:23 *RSVCE*)." "In the seventh year (Ezra 7:7 *RSVCE*)" of King Artaxerxes, Ezra returns to Jerusalem with several families and once there he instructs and exhorts his people to be faithful to Mosaic law. One essential way Ezra ensured observance was by requiring the Jewish men who had returned from exile to leave their non-Jewish wives.

[3]

Bergsma and Pitre argue that Ezra issued directed this harsh order because of his strong sense of social justice:

[3] Gustave Doré [Public domain], "Ezra Reads the Law to the People, one of Gustave Doré's illustrations for La Grande Bible de Tours," https://commons.wikimedia.org/wiki/File:109.Ezra_Reads_the_Law_to_the_People.jpg.

> It was primarily the upper classes of Judean society - "officials," "chief men," priests, and Levites (Ezra 9:1-2) - who were intermarrying with non-Jewish inhabitants. … Furthermore, the choice of the leading male citizens to marry non-Jewish wives left devout Jewish women without eligible spouses, facing a painful choice between a life of practical widowhood or marriage to a foreigner and the resulting loss of religion, culture, and family identity. High-born men were placing their own personal interests above that of their community and especially of its women. It is a naïve imposition of modern categories to think the marriages of the Jewish leaders with foreign women was the result of romantic attachment. Instead, such marriages were contracted for political, social, and economic reasons, most likely to ally upper-class Jews with the leadership classes of surrounding peoples, creating an intermingled, elite ruling caste for the entire region. The losers in this arrangement would be the common Jews (cf. Neh. 5:1-13) and those who took seriously the worship of the Lord according to the Mosaic covenant. … In traditional societies… marriage is a public institution with important social-justice consequences for the entire community.[4]

Nehemiah

"[I]n the twentieth year of King Artaxerxes (Nehemiah 2:1 *RSVCE*)," Nehemiah is serving as a cupbearer to the king. Upon being

---

[4] Bergsma and Pitre, 454.

served wine by Nehemiah, the king asks, "Why is your face sad (Nehemiah 2:2 *RSVCE*)." Nehemiah then tells the king that he is sad because his beloved city of Jerusalem is in ruins and he wishes to "rebuild it (Nehemiah 2:5 *RSVCE*)." The king graciously respects Nehemiah's desire, appoints him governor of Judah (Nehemiah 5:14) and sends him to Jerusalem to rebuild its walls, and restore the city and Temple.

[5]

In Jerusalem, Nehemiah oversees the rebuilding of the Jerusalem's wall. He also collaborates with Ezra in ensuring the people know the Mosaic law: "And they read from the book, from the law of God, clearly; and they gave the sense. So that the people understood the

---

[5] Hult, Adolf, 1869-1943; Augustana synod. [from old catalog] [No restrictions], "Nehemiah rebuilding Jerusalem," https://commons.wikimedia.org/wiki/File:Bible_primer,_Old_Testament,_for_use_in_the_primary_department_of_Sunday_schools_(1919)_(14779759334).jpg.

reading (Nehemiah 8:8 RSVCE)." Helping the people to understand the reading likely meant translating the Hebrew original of the Bible into Aramaic since while the Jewish people were in captivity in Babylon they had adopted Aramaic, the language of their oppressors. This was reflected also in the alphabet that was used by the Jewish people. Prior to the Babylonian captivity, a similar but different alphabet (Paleo-Hebrew) was used. During and after the Babylonian captivity the Aramaic alphabet was used by the Jewish people.[6]

In restoring Jewish culture, Ezra and Nehemiah encourage the Jewish people to repent from breaking the law, and make an amendment to follow the law without grieving since "joy of the Lord" is their "strength (Nehemiah 8:10 *RSVCE*)." Pronounced joy is described as taking place within liturgical celebrations. For example, when Ezra instructs the people to keep the Feast of Booths, the people do so with "very great rejoicing (Nehemiah 8:17 *RSVCE*)." Booths, also known as Tabernacles, and *Sukkot*, is a feast in which the Jewish people live in quickly made booths as a reminder of their ancestors' flight out of Egypt and into the desert.

At the time of Ezra and Nehemiah, as in the time of the Exile, the Jewish people were economically poor, almost powerless politically[7],

---

[6] Robert D. Miller II, *Understanding the Old Testament* (Chantilly: The Teaching Company, 2019), 227-228.

[7] Miller, 227-228. "The restored Jewish community in Judah was by no means independent, nor would it be for centuries. It was a province of the Persian empire until the late 4th century, when it became a province of Alexander the Great's empire. What scholars call the postexilic period—spanning the time from 539 down into the Roman period—was one in which the people of Judah were subject to others. Not oppressed: they never

and experienced few creaturely comforts and yet, surprisingly, they rejoice. The reason for the joy, comments Bergsma and Pitre, was due to their remembering the past not with resentment but with gratitude for God having repeatedly rescued them from difficulties; in addition the joy was due to the Jewish people's hope that someday in the future God will save them in totally perfect manner.[8] The most suitable place for joyful gratitude for the past and joyful hope in the future is, affirms Bergsma and Pitre, the liturgy since this liturgical experiences was and is a privileged moment when heaven kisses earth, when time meets eternity, when those celebrating experience the eternal now of God who encompasses and transcends past, present and future.

Benedict XVI provides another explanation that well applies to the Jewish people's joyful liturgical celebration of the law. In reference to Cardinal Newman, Benedict teaches that true law is related to joy since both are related to an experience of freedom. He argues that authorities who uphold true laws, which reflect the truth of God, are not a "constraint on, threat to…freedom"[9] but rather are precisely the opposite. Obeying laws that reflects God's truth is to be a joyful experience since such laws are in accordance with the truth inscribed by God in our created nature which reflects God's nature. The more these laws are followed, the greater inner freedom, experienced as

---

rebelled against the Persians, but certainly not independent, and after Alexander the Great, under the Greeks, things got progressively worse and somewhat more oppressive. Independence for the Jews was never an option. They were a small, powerless people."

[8] Bergsma and Pitre, 457.

[9] Joseph Ratzinger, *On Conscience: Two Essays*, trans. (San Francisco: Ignatius Press, 2007), 24.

peace and joy, is experienced as the actions of the creature become less and less alienated from, less in contradiction with how we have been created by God to live.

After governing Judah for twelve years (Nehemiah 5:14), Nehemiah leaves Jerusalem to serve King Artaxerxes. This is followed by Nehemiah returning to Jerusalem and there discovering his people have returned to their unfaithful ways, including withholding tithes to the priests, working on the Sabbath, and Jewish men intermarrying with non-Jewish women.

Bergsma and Pitre indicate that the sadness which the last chapter of the book of Nehemiah leaves the reader with is also mixed with an element of implicit hope, hope that one day the people of Judah will be able to follow the laws of the covenant.[10] This ability to follow the law is prophesied by Ezekiel with, "A new heart I will give you, and a new spirit I will put within you; and I will take out of your flesh the heart of stone and give you a heart of flesh (Ezekiel 36:26 *RSVCE*)."

Ezekiel's prophecy, the Catholic Church teaches, is fulfilled in Jesus, who by taking our flesh while remaining God, has offered to all the possibility of loving with His divine heart, thinking with his divine mind, and abiding by his divine spirit. Only by relying on the grace of Jesus, the divine relationship that Jesus offers us is the law, the truth that our minds, hearts, and souls, at their deepest level want to follow, capable of being followed, and the result is deep peace and joy of living in accordance with our created natures.

---

[10] Bergsma and Pitre, 453.

Section Questions

1. Identify in a specific sense Zerubbabel, Ezra, and Nehemiah. Include the following in your response: Rebuilds Jerusalem's Walls, Priest, Temple Rebuilt, Leave Non-Jewish Wives

Tobit

Introduction

The Hebrew based title, Tobit (*Tovi* טובי), comes from introductory verse, "The book of the acts of Tobit (Tobit 1:1 *RSVCE*)." Tobit's name originates out of the Hebrew three letter root *tov* (טוב), good. Almost all of Hebrew is based on three letter roots like *tov*. When letters and vowels are added to the root, the root's meaning changes but not in an essential manner.[1] For example, as Bergsma and Pitre point out, the name of Tobit's son, Tobiah (טוֹבִיָּה) retains the meaning goodness but with an addition of yah (יָּה), an abbreviated form for God's name *Yahweh*. His name means, consequently, "The LORD [God] is good … or… The LORD is my good."[2]

The book focuses on how God manifests his goodness to three people who, although good, nonetheless suffer misfortune: Tobit, Tobias and Sarah.

Tobit

As just stated, the book opens by referring to the "acts of Tobit

---

[1] Michael Carasik, *Biblical Hebrew: Learning a Sacred Language* (Chantilly: The Teaching Company, 2018), 16.

[2] John Bergsma and Brant Pitre, *A Catholic Introduction to the Bible, Volume I* (San Francisco: Ignatius Press, 2018), 462.

(Tobit 1:1 *RSVCE*)" a member of the northern tribe of Naphtali, one of the first tribes to be deported by the Assyrians in 722 B.C. Prior to the deportation, Tobit is described as refusing to break the First Commandment by worshiping the false God Baal whom members from all northern tribes were doing. Instead, along with a few other northern tribe members (Tobit 5:13), Tobit traveled south to Jerusalem to worship God truthfully.

When the northern Kingdom of Israel is defeated by the Assyrians, Tobit is deported by the Assyrians to the capital city of Nineveh. The king at the time, Shalmaneser selected Tobit to be "his buyer of provisions (Tobit 1:13 *RSVCE*)," but when Shalmaneser died he was succeeded by his son Sennacherib, responsible for killing many Judeans. Tobit responded to the killing of the Judeans by reverently and secretly burying the dead. He also cared for his kinsmen in a number of other ways, including feeding the hungry and clothing the naked.

Upon being reported to King Sennacherib for burying the dead without permission from the King, Tobit flees Nineveh and hides. In anger, the King seized Tobit's property. As a consequence, Tobit, his wife Anna and his son Tobias had practically nothing of their own (Tobit 1:16-20).

King Sennacherib's penchant for violence caused him to be disliked by many and even hated by his two of his own sons who eventually killed him. One of his sons, Esarhaddon, then became king. A nephew of Tobit, Ahikar, became the cupbearer to King Esarhaddon and at an opportune time asked the King to be merciful to Tobit. The King agreed and Tobit returned with his wife and son to Nineveh.

Soon after returning home, Tobit once again properly buried one of his own kinsmen and since he had become impure by coming in contact with a dead body (Numbers 19:16) he did not sleep in his bed but instead sleeps outside by a courtyard wall. While sleeping, bird droppings land on his eyes; his eyes become infected, and Tobit becomes blind, no longer able to work and provide for his family. Blind and frustrated, Tobit argues with his wife, accusing her of wrongdoing that she was not guilty of, and she accuses him of rash judgment by being a know it all (Tobit 2:14). In deep grief, Tobit cries out to God that "it is better for me to die than to see so much distress in my life and listen to such insults (Tobit 3:6 *RSVCE*)

Section Questions

1. What was the specific liturgical reason for Tobit's refusal to worship in Northern Kingdom of Israel?

2. What city was Tobit deported to?

3. Why did Tobit bury the dead and how is this specifically related to Tobit fleeing from his home?

4. Where, why and how specifically did Tobit become blind?

Tobias and Sarah

Tobit's prayer to God is followed by an introduction to Sarah who like Tobit is experiencing great suffering but for no apparent fault of her own. Sarah was tortured by a demon who had killed seven men she had consecutively married. Every one of Sarah's seven husbands were killed by the demon before any one of them consummated the marriage. Instead of blaming the demon, Sarah's maids rashly accused Sarah of killing her husbands. Like Tobit, Sarah also prays to God that "I may die and not listen to these reproaches anymore (Tobit 3:10 *RSVCE*)."

The humiliating experiences of Tobit and Sarah lead them almost to despair, which, as Fr. Rolheiser well explains, is always a risk for those who experience humiliations, failure and a sense of being powerless when facing evil. Rolheiser writes:

> just like power and success, failure and humiliation are also dangerous. Power can corrupt, but so can powerlessness. Many are the acts of violence that issue forth when people feel powerless and humiliated. Sometimes failure and frustration build character, but sometimes they build monsters and murderers. Feelings of inferiority drive us into the deeper parts of our souls, but demons, not just angels, lurk in those depths.[3]

The choice facing both Tobit and Sarah was not so much to suffer or not to suffer but rather to suffer, in the words of Rolheiser, "without resentment," without anger, without bitterness or to suffer in peace, believing in God's providence, and "accepting" the feeling of "humiliation and powerlessness ... as a gift that can be used to give something deeper back to the community."[4] Jesus sacrifice on Calvary

---

[3] Ron Rolheiser, "Gethsemane – A Place to Learn A Lesson," February 13, 2005, ronrolheiser.com, http://ronrolheiser.com/gethsemane-a-place-to-learn-a-lesson/#.XLuTDC-ZNhF.

[4] Rolheiser, "Gethsemane – A Place to Learn A Lesson."

is the prime example for how to suffer without even a trace of bitterness, or resentment but rather with complete, unconditional love and trust in His Heavenly Father.

In response to the imperfect suffering of Tobit and Sarah, which anticipates the perfect suffering of Jesus, God intervenes, but, as pointed out by Bergsma and Pitre, not directly.[5] Instead, God sends the angel Raphael to mediate His providential care to those who are suffering. Like God, Raphael also does not directly cure Tobit's blindness and banish the demon from Sarah. Rather, Raphael disguised as a man, befriends Tobit's son Tobias and includes Tobias in his healing mission.

Tobias meets Raphael, disguised as one of Tobias' relatives, when looking for a person to accompany him to Media where he is to collect money that his father had left with Gabael of Rages, Media (Tobit 4:1). His father also tells him to find a wife from among his kinsmen. Raphael leads Tobias not only to Media but also to Sarah who is living in Media and his relative. Before reaching Media Tobias and Raphael camp by the side of the Tigris river. Upon entering the water to bathe, Tobias encounters a large fish that attempts to swallow him.

Raphael tells Tobias to, "Catch the fish (Tobit 6:3 *RSVCE*)" which Tobias does and then throws it on the river-bank. Once again heeding the words of Raphael, Tobias cuts up the fish, and after removing the fish's heart, liver, and gall, roasts and eats the fish. When Tobias asks Raphael, "what use is the liver and heart and gall of the fish?" Raphael explains that the fish's heart, and liver if cooked will give off a smoke that will drive away a demon. In addition, the gall can be made into healing ointment for the blind (Tobit 6:6-8 *RSVCE*).

---

[5] Bergsma and Pitre, 466.

6

As is evident, as God's messenger, Raphael wanted to heal both Sarah from her demonic troubles, and Tobit from his blindness. Respecting the principle of mediation, Raphael does so by ensuring this healing takes place through the creation, especially through another human person, Tobias. In commenting on God's ordinary way of relating us through others, Benedict XVI writes, "our relationship to God and our fellowship with man cannot be separated from each other; the relationship to God, to the 'You', and to the 'We' are intertwined; they do not stand alongside each other."[7] Benedict adds, "The same thing could be formulated … by saying that God

[6] William-Adolphe Bouguereau [Public domain], "*Tobias Saying Good-Bye to his Father.* Painting by William-Adolphe Bouguereau (1860)," https://commons.wikimedia.org/wiki/File:William-Adolphe_Bouguereau_(1825-1905)_-_Tobias_Saying_Good-Bye_to_his_Father_(1860).png.

[7] Joseph Ratzinger, *Introduction to Christianity (Revised Edition)*, trans. J.R. Foster (San Francisco: Ignatius Press, 2004), 93-94.

wishes to approach man only through man; he seeks out man in no other way but in his fellow humanity."[8] We, as Pope Francis repeatedly has taught, go back to God through one another, especially by serving the poor and most vulnerable.

[9]

Sarah is the first to be freed from her ailment by Tobias'

[8] Ratzinger, *Introduction to Christianity (Revised Edition)*, 93-94.

[9] Gustave Doré [Public domain], "*Tobias and the Angel* by Gustave Doré," https://commons.wikimedia.org/wiki/File:110.Tobias_and_the_Angel.jpg.

participation in God's healing mission. First, Tobias is betrothed to Sarah. Then, before consummating his marriage with Sarah, Tobias follows Raphael's instructions and burns the fish's heart and liver so that they smoke. In response to the smoke, which can be understood as representing Tobias's obedience to God's providence, the demon leaves Sarah. With the demon gone, Tobias safely enters into an intimate relationship with his wife Sarah without risk of harm from the demon. Even though the demon has fled, Tobias still refrains from having marital intercourse with Sarah until they have prayed together. Tobias concludes his prayer with Sarah with, "And now, O Lord, I am not taking this sister of mine because of lust, but with sincerity. Grant that I my find mercy and may grow old together with her (Tobit 8:7 *RSVCE*)

Anticipating that Tobias would suffer the same fate of death as Sarah's previous seven husbands had, Sarah's father Raguel digs a grave to Tobias, but when he finds out that Tobias is alive and well, he has the grave filled back in and then throws a fourteen day wedding feast (Tobit 8:19). During the celebration, Tobias sends Raphael to collect the money that Tobit had left with Gabael. After the celebration has concluded and Tobit has his father's money, Tobit returns home with his new wife Sarah.

Upon returning home, Tobias greets his father and then smears on his father's eyes the ointment made from gall of the fish, and Tobit is able to see once again. Seeing that he has completed his mission from God, Raphael then reveals his angelic identity as "one of the seven holy angels who present the prayers of the saints and enter into the presence of the glory of the Lord (Tobit 12:15 *RSVCE*)."

[10]

Section Questions

1. How specifically did Tobit and Sarah pray in a similar way when they faced great suffering?

2. Tobias was accompanied by Raphael. What is Raphael's true identity? With specific reference to the principle of mediation, Benedict XVI, and Pope Francis why didn't Raphael miraculously heal Sarah and Tobit immediately and directly?

---

[10] Domingos Sequeira [Public domain], "*Tobias heals the blindness of his father Tobit*, by Domingos Sequeira," https://commons.wikimedia.org/wiki/File:Tobias_cura_a_cegueira_de_seu_pai_-_Domingos_Sequeira.png.

Typology

Bergsma and Pitre describe Tobias and Sarah as anticipating Jesus, the New Adam, and Mary, the New Eve. As the sinless new Adam and sinless new Eve, Jesus and Mary bring mankind back to its beginning before the Fall. By so doing, Jesus and Mary heal the rupture between God and humanity caused by old Adam and old Eve who passed on Original Sin. Unlike the old Adam, who failed to protect his bride Eve, Jesus laid down his life for his Church, perfectly embodied in the immaculately conceived Mary. Foreshadowing the sacrifice of Jesus for his bride the Church, Tobias protects Sarah from a demon even to the extent of risking his life for her.[11]

[12]

[11] Bergsma and Pitre, 466.

[12] Julius Schnorr von Carolsfeld [Public domain], "*Tobias and Sara Sleep*, 1860 woodcut by Julius Schnorr von Karolsfeld," https://commons.

Tobias' exemplary, sacrificial love for his wife Sarah anticipates Christ's presence in yet another way, anticipating Christ's presence extended sacramentally through time especially through the Sacrament of Matrimony. By being open to life, by raising children, by being united life-long in marriage to one another, and by being temperate with respect to sexual desire, Tobias and Sarah are models with respect to the primary end of marriage of procreation, and the secondary end of union.[13] Their marriage points to the Sacrament of Marriage through which in Christ the two couples are to live out, in the words of Pius XI, the "chief reason" of marriage, sanctification and perfection of one another.[14] This sanctification in Christ, where in participation of Christ's total, unreserved gift of himself to His Church, the bride of Christ, the spouses are to be signs of God's spousal love in the world (Ephesians 5:32), as beautifully taught by John Paul II.

> Christ has become the spouse of the Church. He has married the Church as a bride, because "He has given himself up for her" (Eph 5:25). Through marriage as a sacrament (as one of the

---

wikimedia.org/wiki/File:Schnorr_von_Carolsfeld_Bibel_in_Bildern_1860_147.png.

[13] See Canon 1013, 1917 Code of Canon Law. Quoted in Crisis Magazine. Jim Russell, "Procreation: Still the Primary End of Marriage," April 25, 2017, crisismagazine.com, https://www.crisismagazine.com/2017/procreation-still-primary-end-marriage.

[14] Pius XI, "*Casti Connubi*, 1930, no. 24," w2.vatican.va, https://w2.vatican.va/content/pius-xi/en/encyclicals/documents/hf_p-xi_enc_19301231_casti-connubii.html.

> sacraments of the Church) both these dimensions of love, the spousal and the redemptive, together with the grace of the sacrament, permeate the life of the spouses. The spousal significance of the body in its masculinity and femininity was manifested for the first time in the mystery of creation against the background of man's original innocence. This significance is linked in the image of the Letter to the Ephesians with the redemptive significance, and in this way, it is confirmed and in a certain sense, "newly created."[15]

This divine, spiritual marriage between Christ and his Church was anticipated by Tobias and Sarah.

Venerable Bede identifies yet another way that Tobias is a type of Christ. Bede's sees typology in the account of the unusually aggressive fish trying to swallow Tobias. The fish, writes Bede, "signifies the ancient devourer of humankind, namely the devil, whom the divine power snared while the devil was eagerly anticipating the death of the flesh in our Redeemer."[16] In contrast with Tobias, and in fulfillment of Tobias, death tried to swallow Jesus and totally dissolve Jesus, but right at the moment when all seemed lost was the exact time when Jesus

---

[15] John Paul II, "The Redemptive and Spousal Dimensions of Love, General Audience of Wednesday, 15 December [1982], no. 4" ewtn.com, https://www.ewtn.com/library/PAPALDOC/JP2TB102.HTM.

[16] Early Church Fathers Bible Commentary on Tobit," Patristic Bible Commentary,
https://sites.google.com/site/aquinasstudybible/home/tobit/early-church-fathers-bible-commentary-on-tobit. The following source is cited. Bede the Venerable, *Allegorica interpretation in Tobiam,* PL 91.928B.

conquered death, sin, and the devil. Jesus did so by rising from the dead since Jesus is God, is eternal life and eternal life, and God cannot die, cannot be touched sin or destroyed by diabolic powers.

Section Questions

1. How did Tobias specifically relate to Sarah in a way that Adam failed to and in a way that anticipates Jesus' relationship to the Church?

Judith

Introduction

The book of Judith is named after the main character, Judith. Her name Judith (יְהוּדִית *Yehudith*) simply means a Jewish woman. Judith belonged to the tribe of Simeon (Judith 9:2). The father of this tribe, Simeon had violently avenged Shechem's rape of Dinah (Genesis 34).

After the rape, Shechem's father boldly asked Jacob and his sons to permit Shechem to marry Dinah. Jacob's sons, including Simeon, claimed that they could not unless Shechem was circumcised. In addition, they insisted, Dinah could not marry Shechem unless all the men of Shechem's people are circumcised. Shechem and the men of his city agreed. Once they were circumcised and incapable of defending themselves, Simeon and Levi killed all the men.

Like her ancestress Dinah, Judith was desired by a man, Holofernes, but unlike Dinah, Judith was not raped but rather killed the man who wanted to possess and cruelly dominate Judith and her people.

It is not clear who Holofernes is and who the king, Nebuchadnezzar is, whom Holofernes served as a military general. The book identifies Nebuchadnezzar as an Assyrian King and yet the Nebuchadnezzar (Nebuchadnezzar II (c.634-c.562 B.C)) who conquered Judah in 587 B.C. was a Babylonian king and not an Assyrian king. Bergsma and Pitre explain that it is possible that the

Babylonian Nebuchadnezzar is implied since after Nebuchadnezzar II's father Nabopolassar had conquered the Assyrians and replaced their empire with a Babylonian empire he also kept their political titles along with the Babylonian titles.[1] Even if this is the case, add Bergsma and Pitre, there still exist other unresolved historical contradictions in the book including describing Judith and "Nebuchadnezzar" living during the reconstruction of the Jerusalem Temple that took place over seventy years after Nebuchadnezzar II had died (Judith 4:3).[2]

[3]

[1] John Bergsma and Brant Pitre, *A Catholic Introduction to the Bible, Volume I* (San Francisco: Ignatius Press, 2018), 481.

[2] Bergsma and Pitre, 481.

[3] James Tissot / Public domain, "Dinah Tissot," https://commons.wikimedia.org/wiki/File:Dinah_tissot.jpg.

Despite these and other discrepancies, Church Fathers have recognized the book as a narration of history. Modern Scripture scholars, explain Bergsma and Pitre, typically do not regard the book of Judith as a historical narrative but rather as "cryptic or historical fiction," or another similar fictional genre, like "historical romance."[4] To what extent the book of Ruth represents historical events will likely not be settled in a decisive manner. What is, though, immediately evident when reading and reflecting on the book, regardless of its literary genre, is how God reveals his identity. As Irene Nowell phrases it, "the central question in this book is "who is God?"[5] This answer to this question is revealed through those, especially Judith, whom God chooses to mediate his salvific will. We will first reflect on Judith's participation in salvation history. By so doing God's identity will be gradually revealed through Judith, where Judith points to her perfect fulfillment in Jesus and Mary.

Section Questions

1. What does the name Judith mean in Hebrew?

Typology

One characteristic of Judith that is immediately evident is that she is a widow. In reference to the Pentateuch, Nowell explains that in

---

[4] Bergsma and Pitre, 482.

[5] Irene Nowell, *Jonah, Tobit, Judith: 25 New Collegeville Bible Commentary: Old Testament* (Collegeville: Liturgical Press, 2015), Kindle Locations 661-663.

ancient Israelite culture widows were "among the most vulnerable persons" along with orphans, and immigrants.[6] Despite being a widow, Judith was prominent and wealthy since she had inherited her late husband's property. She was also known for her beauty and intelligence. Judith placed at the service of God all of these mentioned qualities. Her beauty coupled with her vulnerability likely caused Holofernes to desire her even more since a woman's apparent need for a protector coupled with beauty sometimes cause certain men to desire a woman like Judith even more since by being the woman's savior the man hopes his social status will increase.

Judith's vulnerability and beauty enabled her to kill Nebuchadnezzar's leading general Holofernes by enchanting him with her beauty, getting him drunk, (he drank "more than he had ever drunk in any one day since he was born (Judith 12:20 *RSVCE*))," and finally by cutting off his head as he lay in drunken stupor. After the beheading, Judith and her maid quietly returned home where they showed off the decapitated head. With a surge of confidence, the Israelites attack the Assyrian army, easily defeating them.

Judith's characteristics of beauty, intelligence, and vulnerability are typologically fulfilled in Christ. First, God use of beauty to save the Israelites is fulfilled in Christ who through his human nature represents the perfect divine beauty of God. Judith's beauty, along with all created beauty, are intended by God to lead to Christ, and through Christ's perfect humanity, to God. As St. Augustine poetically phrases

---

[6] Irene Nowell, *Jonah, Tobit, Judith: 25 New Collegeville Bible Commentary: Old Testament* (Collegeville: Liturgical Press, 2015), Kindle Locations 812-816. Nowell cites (Exodus 22:21-22; Deuteronomy 14:29; 24:17-21; 26:12-13; 27:19).

it:

[7]

> Question the beauty of the earth, question the beauty of the sea, question the beauty of the air, amply spread around everywhere, question the beauty of the sky, question the serried ranks of the stars, question the sun making the day glorious with its bright beams, question the moon tempering the darkness of the following night with its shining rays, question the animals that move in the waters, that amble about on dry land, that fly in the air; their souls hidden, their bodies evident; the visible bodies needing to be controlled, the

[7] Julius Schnorr von Carolsfeld [Public domain], "*Judith Returns to Bethulia*, 1860 woodcut by Julius Schnorr von Karolsfeld," https://commons.wikimedia.org/wiki/File:Schnorr_von_Carolsfeld_Bibel_in_Bildern_1860_145.png.

> invisible souls controlling them; question all these things. They all answer you, 'Here we are, look; we're beautiful.' Their beauty is their confession. Who made these beautiful changeable things, if not one who is beautiful and unchangeable?[8]

Sadly, we often mistakenly think that the created beautiful goods of this world will satisfy us and, as Augustine points out, they cannot since our hearts are made for the origin and end of all, who is God the most beautiful one. "[O]ur hearts are restless," writes Augustine, "till they find rest in Thee," God, till the find rest in the source of all beauty, of all that is desired.[9] As the our ultimate end, God desires to save us from our disordered loves which cause us to confuse an earthly good with God. Through Jesus, the bridge between Heaven and earth, we are saved by the misery, strife, and warfare caused by our disordered loves. As a perfect image of God, Jesus is, in the words of Dostoyevsky, "the beauty that will save the world."[10] Dostoyevsky further writes,

---

[8] Augustine, "Sermons, 241, Easter: c. 411 A.D.," vatican.va, http://www.vatican.va/spirit/documents/spirit_20000721_agostino_en.html.

[9] Augustine, *The Confessions of St. Augustin*, trans. J.G. Pilkington, ed. Philip Schaff, *The Confessions and Letters of St. Augustin with a Sketch of His Life and Work* (Buffalo, NY: Christian Literature Company, 1886), 45.

[10] The actual translation given is "that beauty saves the world." Fyodor Dostoyevsky, *The Idiot*, trans. Frederick Whishaw (London: Vizetelly & Co., 1887), 257; "Beauty for Dostoevsky is thus essentially moral beauty; and it is significant that he regarded Jesus Christ, for him the highest personification of the moral ideal, in aesthetic terms. "There is only one positively beautiful figure in the world, Christ," he wrote to Apollon Maikov in 1868, "and so the

"There is only one positively beautiful figure in the world, Christ and so the appearance of this immeasurably, infinitely beautiful figure is of course an infinite miracle."[11]

In commenting on Dostoyevsky's often quoted verse on beauty saving the world, Benedict XVI reminds us that Christ's beauty is paradoxical, since Christ's life, especially when Christ was crucified, is terrifying and even repellant to behold while at the same time, due to the perfectly morally true, divine love that underlies Christ's passion, most beautiful to behold.

After ascending into heaven and sending the Holy Spirit into the Church, Christ's life of paradoxical beauty is lived out through his Mystical Body, above all through the life of Mary and the saints. As Benedict XVI writes, "Nothing can bring us into close contact with the beauty of Christ himself other than the world of beauty created by faith and light that shines out from the faces of the saints, through whom his own light becomes visible."[12]

The perfect truthful beauty of Christ's life was anticipated by

---

appearance of this immeasurably, infinitely beautiful figure is of course an infinite miracle (28.2:251)." K.A. Lantz, *The Dostoevsky Encyclopedia* (Westport: Greenwood Press, 2004), 7-8.

[11] Lantz, 7-8.

"Beauty for Dostoevsky is thus essentially moral beauty; and it is significant that he regarded Jesus Christ, for him the highest personification of the moral ideal, in aesthetic terms. "There is only one positively beautiful figure in the world, Christ," he wrote to Apollon Maikov in 1868, "and so the appearance of this immeasurably, infinitely beautiful figure is of course an infinite miracle (28.2:251)."

[12] Benedict XVI, *Day by Day with Pope Benedict XVI*, ed. Peter John Cameron (San Francisco: Ignatius Press, 2006), 240.

beautiful people like Judith. In achieving victory over Holofernes in heroic but also imperfect manner, Judith points to Mary and Jesus who perfectly defeat evil.

[13]

Unlike Mary, Judith used lies as a way to defeat the Assyrians. The *Catechism of the Catholic Church* clearly condemns all lies, including lies like Judith's which was said for a noble purpose. "A good intention (for example, that of helping one's neighbor)" states the *Catechism* "does not make behavior that is intrinsically disordered, such as lying and calumny, good or just. The end does not justify the means (*CCC* 1753)."[14] In applying this teaching to Judith, Bergsma and Pitre refer

[13] Julius Schnorr von Carolsfeld [Public domain], "Julius Schnorr von Carolsfeld (1860)," https://commons.wikimedia.org/wiki/File:Schnorr_von_Carolsfeld_Bibel_in_Bildern_1860_144.png.

[14] "Catechism of the Catholic Church," vatican.va, http://www.vatican.va/archive/ENG0015/__P5R.HTM, no. 1753.

to Aquinas who acknowledges that Judith is to be praised "not for lying to Holofernes, but for her desire to save the people, to which end she exposed herself to danger." Aquinas, then adds, "And yet one might also say that her words contain truth in some mystical sense."[15] Due to the "inspired nature of Scripture" Aquinas, explain Bergsma and Pitre, "admits that there may also be some spiritual meaning to her words that transcends the literal meaning of the text."[16]

[17]

[15] Aquinas, "*Summa Theologiae*," newdvent.org, http://www.newadvent.org/summa/3110.htm, II-II, q. 110, art. 3, ad. 3; John Bergsma and Brant Pitre, *A Catholic Introduction to the Bible, Volume I* (San Francisco: Ignatius Press, 2018), 483.

[16] John Bergsma and Brant Pitre, *A Catholic Introduction to the Bible, Volume I* (San Francisco: Ignatius Press, 2018), 483.

[17] Julius Schnorr von Carolsfeld [Public domain], "*Judith Returns to Bethulia*, 1860 woodcut by Julius Schnorr von Karolsfeld," https://commons.wikimedia.org/wiki/File:Schnorr_von_Carolsfeld_Bibel_in_Bildern_1860_145.png.

Another difference is that although Judith was relatively defenseless, due to Judith's status as a woman and widow, she was much less vulnerable than Mary was since Judith was wealthy and had some prominence. Mary, on the other hand, was one of the defenseless poor and experienced powerlessness and defenselessness repeatedly in her life in ways that Judith did not. Mary experienced intense vulnerability early on by being pregnant when only "betrothed to Joseph, before they came together (Matthew 1:18 *RSVCE*)," by being deemed so unimportant that she could not find a room to stay even though she was pregnant, and by fleeing to Egypt.

Despite Mary greater experience of vulnerability, defenselessness, and powerlessness she never resorted to using evil means, such as lying, for a good end, to protect herself and her child. Judith, though, did resort to using an evil means, lying, for a good end, saving her people. In addition, Mary did not aim at rescuing her people from political oppression, as Judith did. Rather, Mary, in cooperation with her son Jesus, helped to redeem all people from greater oppressive forces: sin and demonic powers. This does not mean that Mary and her son Jesus did not care about political oppression. They certainly did, but the Father's will for them was that they redeem people by primarily suffering with them, and through this suffering offering them hope that their suffering can be transformed by the resurrected life of Jesus Christ who was crucified by the Romans and rose from the dead. As Fr. Rolheiser well explains:

> It took the early Christians some time to grasp that Jesus doesn't ordinarily give special exemptions to his friends, no more than God gave special exemptions to Jesus. So, like us,

they struggled with the fact that someone can have a deep, genuine faith, be deeply loved by God, and still have to suffer humiliation, pain, and death like everyone else. God didn't spare Jesus from suffering and death, and Jesus doesn't spare us from them.

That is one of the key revelations inside of the resurrection and is the one we perhaps most misunderstand. We are forever predicating our faith on, and preaching, a rescuing God, a God who promises special exemptions to those of genuine faith: Have a genuine faith in Jesus, and you will be spared from life's humiliations and pains! Have a genuine faith in Jesus, and prosperity will come your way! Believe in the resurrection, and rainbows will surround your life!

Would it were so! But Jesus never promised us rescue, exemptions, immunity from cancer, or escape from death. He promised rather that, in the end, there will be redemption, vindication, immunity from suffering, and eternal life. But that's in the end; meantime, in the early and intermediate chapters of our lives, there will be the same kinds of humiliation, pain, and death that everyone else suffers.

The death and resurrection of Jesus reveal a redeeming, not a rescuing, God.[18]

---

[18] Ron Rolheiser, "The Resurrection as Revealing God as Redeemer, not Rescuer," ronrolheiser.com, http://ronrolheiser.com/the-resurrection-as-revealing-god-as-redeemer-not-as-rescuer/#.Woy_CWa-Ki5

Section Questions

1. Compare and contrast Judith with Mary. In your response include the following in a specific manner: Holofernes, Genesis 3:15, Beauty, Lying, Poverty, Salvation, Political Liberation

Esther

Introduction

The book of Esther takes placed during the reign of a Persian king identified as Ahasuerus.[1] King Ahasuerus is commonly referred to by his Greek name, Xerxes I (519-465 B.C.). Xerxes I is particularly known for invading Greece in 480 B.C. only to be defeated. The book of Esther begins with King Ahasuerus angrily deposing Queen Vashti. Vashti had greatly upset him by refusing to display her beauty at a banquet the king was hosting. The king's counselors urged him to punish Vashti by taking the queenship away from her and giving this position to someone more worthy lest, in imitation of Vashti's disobedience, women throughout the Persian empire will "look with contempt upon their husbands (Esther 1:17 *RSVCE*)." The king does so and initiates process of finding a new queen.

Eventually, a young Jewish woman is chosen who among the gentiles is known as Esther and whose Hebrew name is Hadassah

---

[1] According to Bergsma and Pitre, "The name Ahasuerus (Hebrew Ăhashwērôsh) is a transliteration of the Persian Xšayaršā, who is known in the West by his Greek name: Xerxes. King Xerxes I, also known as Xerxes "the Great" (519-465 B.C.), was the much-feared enemy of the Greeks in the ancient histories of Herodotus and Thucydides." John Bergsma and Brant Pitre, *A Catholic Introduction to the Bible, Volume I* (San Francisco: Ignatius Press, 2018), 490.

(הֲדַסָּה), meaning myrtle, a small flowing tree (Esther 1:7). Due to the early death of her parents, Esther was raised by her uncle, Mordecai, a court official. Like Esther, Mordecai had a non-Hebrew name. Unlike Esther, though, Mordecai's Hebrew name is not given. Their non-Hebrew names likely originate from two important Babylonian Gods: Ishtar and Marduk.

[2]

When Esther is chosen to be queen both she and her uncle work directly for the king in his court. In commenting on these two "court

---

[2] Edwin Long [Public domain], "Painting by en:Edwin Long, 1878. Location of painting: National Gallery of Victoria, Melbourne," https://commons.wikimedia.org/wiki/File:Esther_haram.jpg.

Jews," Irving Greenberg writes, that "court Jews…were typically half-Gentile in their ways of living. When Mordecai asked Esther to plead with the king, she vacillated at first-just the reaction one would expect from a marginal Jew who was reluctant to lose her place in society."[3] Nonetheless, Greenberg adds, "the evidence points to Mordecai's and Esther's being devoted Jews; usually it takes that type to risk their lives to save their people. The rabbinic tradition very strongly insists that they were observant Jews."[4] The text tends to support this tradition, in particular, notes Greenberg, by Esther's request for her people to turn to God with intercessory fasting (Esther 4:16).[5]

[6]

[3] Irving Greenberg, *The Jewish Way* (New York: Touchstone, 1988), 227-228.

[4] Greenberg, 228.

[5] Greenberg, 228.

[6] Julius Schnorr von Carolsfeld [Public domain], "Esther is crowned in this 1860 woodcut by Julius Schnorr von Karolsfeld," https://commons.wikimedia.org/wiki/File:Schnorr_von_Carolsfeld_Bibel_in_Bildern_1860_129.png.

Esther asks the Jewish people to fast after the high-ranking court official Haman, in envy of Mordecai, had persuaded the king to sign a letter by which Jewish people throughout the Persian realm would be mercilessly killed. Desiring to save her people, Esther prays and fasts for three days and then dares to approach the king, even though she has not been called by him. Seeing Esther, the king reacts "in fierce anger (Esther 15:7 *RSVCE*)" to which the queen responds by fainting. Quickly changing his disposition, the king rushes from his throne to comfort Esther and Esther invites him to a special dinner. He agrees and at the dinner Esther denounces Haman for plotting to destroy her people. When the king leaves the dinner, Haman begs Esther to spare his life while holding onto to the couch that Esther was reclining in. Upon returning, the king sees Haman and accuses Haman of attempting "to assault the queen in my presence in my own house (Esther 7:8 *RSVCE*)" Shortly afterwards, by order of the king, Haman is hanged, and the king issues another letter, permitting the Jewish people, "to live under their own laws," and, "to defend themselves against those who attack them (Esther 16:19-20 *RSVCE*)."

 [7]

[7] Ernest Normand [Public domain], "*Esther Denouncing Haman* by Ernest Normand," https://commons.wikimedia.org/wiki/File:Esther_Denouncing_Haman.jpg.

Section Questions

1. What is a specific reason that the book of Esther gives for Queen Vashti losing her queenship?

Providence

To decide when the Jewish people would die Haman played a game of chance "Pur (פּוּר) (Esther 3:7)," meaning lots. Chance determined that Jewish people would die in the month of Adar. The joyful Jewish festival of Purim, meaning lots, celebrates God acting through Esther and Mordecai to save His people (Esther 9:17).

The celebration of Purim is a joyful affirmation that behind all disorder, chaos and chance is a God of love who upholds all in existence and who subtly draws good out of even the most awful of circumstances. The ultimate expression of this typically hidden divine action is the crucifixion of Jesus which at first sight seemed to indicate to Jesus' followers that what is most essential to the world, is chaos, violence, and chance. However, upon rising on the third day Jesus revealed God's truthful, abiding love is the most essential reality, as the reality that simply is, and is greater than all evil violence that has and will take place.

The punishment that Haman receives, impaled on the pole that he had set up to kill Mordecai on, is a visible sign of what Galatians teaches, "Do not be deceived; God is not mocked, for whatever a man sows, that he will also reap (Galatian 6:7 *RSVCE*)." This literally applied to Haman in his lifetime and may apply, if there is no repentance, to others eternally after they die.

Section Questions

1. What is the game that Haman played to determine when the Jewish people will die and how is this related to God's Providence? Include in your response the following: Pur, Chance, Chaos, Providence.

Typology

Esther prefigures Mary. In writing on Esther as a type of Mary, John Paul II, comment Bergsma and Pitre, contrasts Judith with Esther:

> Judith and Esther both risk their lives to win the salvation of their people. The two interventions [which anticipate Mary's mission], however, are quite different: Esther does not kill the enemy but, by playing the role of mediator, intercedes for those who are threatened with destruction.[8]

By killing her people's enemy, Judith anticipated Mary's collaborative role with her offspring in crushing the head of Satan (Genesis 3:15). Mary's offspring is Jesus who is present through the Church, Christ's presence extended through time. As members of the

---

[8] John Paul II, "Woman's Indispensable Role in Salvation History," March 27, 1996, ewtn.com, http://www.ewtn.com/library/PAPALDOC/JP2BVM15.HTM; Bergsma and Pitre, 502.

Church, we are invited to participate in Jesus' defeat of evil.

Esther foreshadows the defeat of evil in a different way than Judith. Unlike Judith, Esther does not directly fight against her people's enemy, instead she goes to the king and begs him to spare her people.

Similarly, but in a perfect sense, Mary intercedes for her people, which is the entire human race, by offering her son as a perfect sacrifice to God. Only because of Christ's perfect sacrifice offered by Mary, can our imperfect efforts and sacrifices be made pleasing to God since they may now be taken up, incorporated in, and transformed by the one perfect sacrifice of Jesus, the one high priest and perfect victim.

Another difference between Esther's intercession and Mary's intercession that Bergsma and Pitre point out is that unlike Esther who interceded only for her people, Mary intercedes for all people.[9]

Section Questions

1. How does Esther foreshadow Mary and how does Mary fulfill Esther's saving role in a way that surpasses Esther's saving role? In your response, include the following: Prayer and Intercession

[9] Bergsma and Pitre, 503.

1 Maccabees and 2 Maccabees

Introduction

The title Maccabees is a name for a priestly, Levitical family named the Hasmoneans who fought against Greek domination. Their name originates from a common name for Judas son of Mattathias, "Judas called Maccabeus (1 Maccabees 2:4 *RSVCE*)." To ensure Jewish independence from Greek rule, Judas Maccabeus allied Israel with Rome (1 Maccabees 8:17). The Hasmonean Dynasty backed by Rome lasted from 135 B.C. to 63 B.C. In 63 B.C., the Roman leader Pompey the Great enforced Roman rule over Jerusalem as Jerusalem was in the midst of a civil war.[1] Finally, in 37 B.C. Rome installed King Herod the Great as King of Judea, the King who reigned when Jesus was born, and who ordered all male babies in Bethlehem two years and younger to be killed since he feared the prophecy that a "king of the Jews (Matthew 2:2 *RSVCE*)" would be born in Bethlehem.

The first chapters of the second book provide historical context for the first book's account of the Maccabees. Chapter three begins by describing the devout high priest of the Jerusalem temple, Onias. Under Onias' pious leadership, there was peace throughout the land. Even the Greek Seleucid kings "honored… and glorified the temple (2 Maccabees 3:2 *RSVCE*)." Sadly, this peace did not last because, out of

---

[1] Scott Hahn, *Catholic Bible Dictionary* (New York: Doubleday, 2009), 344.

spite, a member from the tribe of Benjamin, Simon, sought to harm the high priest Onias with whom he had an argument with. Simon did so by falsely reporting to the Greek Seleucid government that the Temple contained great wealth, wealth that could be put at the service of the Greek empire.

In response, the Greek Seleucid emperor, Seleucus, sends Heliodorus along with troops to seize these funds for the king's treasury. Heliodorus is prevented from doing so by angels sent to defend the Temple. The reason given for this angelic defense is because of the high priest Onias' holiness and devotion to the God (2 Maccabees 3:33 *RSVCE*). This miraculous protection of the Temple ends when Onias is replaced by his brother Jason who "obtained the high priesthood by corruption (2 Maccabees 4:7 *RSVCE*)." The corruption involved promising the new Greek Seleucid emperor, Antiochus, money and the establishment of Greek customs in Jerusalem. Jason himself becomes a victim of corruption when the brother of Simon the Benjaminite, Menelaus, bribes Emperor Antiochus with "three hundred talents of silver (2 Maccabees 4:24 *RSVCE*)."

Supported by Emperor Antiochus, Menelaus assumes the office of the high priesthood and Jason flees. Jason' brother, Onias, who had previously held the high priesthood, publicly denounces Menelaus evil ways, in particular for stealing gold from the Temple and giving it to Andronicus. In response, Menelaus, persuades Andronicus to kill Onias. Dismayed by the murder of a just, holy man, who as high priest maintained peace in Jerusalem, the Jewish people appeal to the Emperor Antiochus. Out of respect for Onias's holy, just reputation, Antiochus has Andronicus killed. Menelaus, though, remained in the office of high priest. In time, Jason comes out of hiding and attempts to take back the high priesthood, in so doing Judea is plunged into civil war.

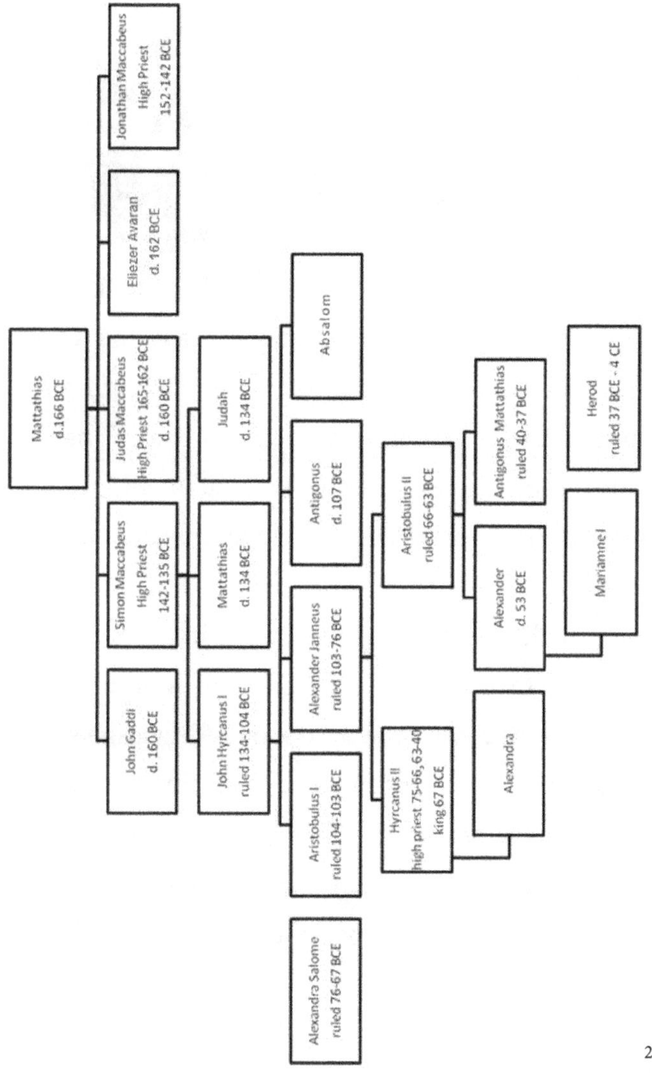

[2]

[2] Marshall46 [CC BY-SA 3.0 (https://creativecommons.org/licenses/by-sa/3.0)], "The descendants of Mattathias," https://commons.wikimedia.org/wiki/File:Maccabean_dynasty.PNG.

[3]

Thinking that Judea was revolting against the Greek empire, Emperor Antiochus responds by storming into Jerusalem with his troops who mercilessly kill many residents, including babies, children and women. Upon violently taking Jerusalem, Emperor Antiochus desecrates the Temple and renames it the temple of Zeus (2 Maccabees 6:2).

Now that the historical context present in 2 Maccabees has been outlined, we will focus on the first book of Maccabees. As broken down by Bergsma and Pitre, the first book of Maccabees describes the Jewish fight for political independence from Emperor Antiochus as a battle to freely practice the Jewish faith. The book begins with an introduction on the division of Alexander the Great's empire among his officers, one of whom rules over the Seleucid Empire.[4] At the time

---

[3] Julius Schnorr von Carolsfeld [Public domain], "*Rider on the Horse* with golden armour, who appears in Chapter 3 to fight Heliodorus, from *Die Bibel in Bildern*," https://commons.wikimedia.org/wiki/File:Schnorr_von_Carolsfeld_Bibel_in_Bildern_1860_156.png.

[4] John Bergsma and Brant Pitre, *A Catholic Introduction to the Bible, Volume I* (San Francisco: Ignatius Press, 2018), 508.

of the Maccabees, in the "one hundred and thirty-seventh year of the kingdom of the Greeks (1 Maccabees 1:10 *RSVCE*)," the Seleucid Empire is ruled by Antiochus IV Epiphanes. Not satisfied with his portion of the Greek empire, Antiochus invades the Egyptian Ptolemaic Greek Empire, conquering much of its lands (1 Maccabees 1:16-19).

Upon traveling back to his Western Seleucid lands, Antiochus stops in Jerusalem while it is in the midst of a civil war. In anger, Antiochus enters the Jerusalem Temple, desecrates it, and renames it the "temple of Olympian Zeus ... (2 Maccabees 6:2 *RSVCE*)." He further desecrates the temple by encouraging prostitution and other acts that are in direct violation with Jewish law. To further undermine observance of the Jewish law, also Antiochus commands the Jewish people to sacrifice pigs and "unclean animals (1 Maccabees 1:47 *RSVCE*)." According to the second book of Maccabees, the day the temple was desecrated was the 25th day of Chislev. Since the Jewish calendar is based on lunar cycles and not solar cycles it is difficult to identify the month of Chislev with a solar month, but it corresponds roughly to November or December.[5]

The introductory chapter is followed, explains Bergsma and Pitre, by a description of the Maccabean heroes, beginning with Maccabean Patriarch Mattathias and then focuses on Mattathias's sons Judas Maccabeus, Jonathan, and Simon. 1 Maccabees ends with the grandson of Mattathias, John Hyrcanus.

Mattathias sparks the Jewish revolt when instead of obeying the Emperor Antiochus Epiphanes's command that the Jews offering

---

[5] MJL, "Months of the Jewish Year," myjewishlearning.com, https://www.myjewishlearning.com/article/months-of-the-jewish-year/.

sacrifice to Greek Gods, he kills the Jewish man willing to break the First Commandment prohibiting idolatry and then kills the emperor's officer. Finally, Mattathias tears down the idolatrous altar and flees into the wilderness with his sons and supporters (1 Maccabees 2:27 *RSVCE*).

[6]

Mattathias is succeeded by his son Judas who inspires six thousand men (2 Maccabees 8:1) to join him in fighting the Greeks. To ensure a greater likelihood of his men successfully resisting the Greek military might, Judas allies the Jewish state with Rome. Supported by this alliance, Judas repeatedly defeats the Greek

---

[6] Phillip Medhurst [FAL], "Mattathias slaying the Jewish apostate, painting by Philippe De Loutherbourg," https://commons.wikimedia.org/wiki/File:Plate_14_of_22_for_the_Macklin_Bible_after_Loutherbourg._Bowyer_Bible._Mattathias_Punishes_Idolatry_2.gif.

Seleucids in battle. Once Judas regains Jerusalem from Greek oppression, he purifies and rededicates the Jerusalem Temple on the very same day of the year that the Greeks had desecrated the Temple, the 25th day of Chislev. This rededication is the origin of the Jewish feast day of Hanukkah.

Eventually, the Greeks defeat Judas' military and kills Judas in battle (1 Maccabees 9:18, 29-30). "After the death of Judas," recounts the first book of Maccabees, "the lawless emerged in all parts of Israel; all the doers of injustice appeared (1 Maccabees 9:23 *RSVCE*)." In response, followers of Judas appoint Judas' brother Jonathan as their new leader.

Building upon his brother's political shrewdness, Jonathan establishes an important political alliance, with a Greek faction led by Alexander Epiphanes who is attempting to overthrow the Greek Seleucid King Demetrius. Strengthened by this alliance, Alexander successfully overthrows Demetrius and takes the throne. Later, Jonathan renews the political alliance his brother had established with the Romans and forms an alliance with the Greek Spartans (1 Maccabees 12). Like his brother, Jonathan dies on the battlefield and is replaced by his brother Simon, the last of the Maccabean brothers (1 Maccabees 13:8).

Simon's rule comes to a tragic end when his son-in-law, Ptolemy, invites Simon to a meal and there kills him along with two of Simon's three sons. After killing the assassins sent by Ptolemy, Simon's remaining son, John Hyrcanus, assumes his father's leadership role as ruler of Judea and as high priest (1 Maccabees 16:24).

We now turn from an historical outline of the books of Maccabees to its theology. The books of Maccabees explicitly refer to several beliefs that are further clarified in the Catholic faith including: creation out of nothing, life after death, prayers for the dead, and bodily Resurrection. These beliefs are related to the dynamic tension within the books of Maccabees between humble, obedient martyrdom for the faith and dying for political change as a political revolutionary.

Section Questions

1. What tribe did the Maccabees belong to?

2. Who was Antiochus and how and why did he specifically desecrate the Jerusalem Temple?

3. How is the 25th day of Chislev significant? Include in your answer the following in a specific sense: Desecration, Rededication, November or December, Hanukkah

4. To defeat the Greeks who did Judas ally his people with?

Martyrdom, Political Revolution, and Priesthood

The belief that God created the world out of nothing (*creatio ex nihilo*) is present in the second book of Maccabees. In encouraging her last and youngest son to refuse to break God's law and be martyred the mother of seven sons says:

> I beseech you, my child, to look at the heaven and the earth and see everything that is in them, and recognize that God did not make them out of things that existed. Thus, also mankind

> comes into being. Do not fear this butcher, but prove worthy of your brothers. Accept death, so that in God's mercy I may get you back again with your brothers (2 Maccabees 7:28 *RSVCE*).

[7]

Belief in life after death and prayers for the dead is evident in the passage from the second book of Maccabees when Judas and his followers retrieve the bodies of those killed on the battlefield. As they did so, it is discovered that every one of the fallen are wearing a false idol under their garments. Maccabees explains, "And it became clear to all that this was why these men had fallen. So, they all blessed the ways of the Lord, the righteous Judge, who reveals the things that are hidden; and they turned to prayer, beseeching that the sin which had been committed might be wholly blotted out (2 Maccabees 12:40-42 *RSVCE*)." This is followed by an even further affirmation of life after death, with references to post-death purification from sin and bodily

---

[7] Julius Schnorr von Carolsfeld [Public domain], "*Martyrs* refusing to sacrifice from *Die Bibel in Bildern*," https://commons.wikimedia.org/wiki/File:Schnorr_von_Carolsfeld_Bibel_in_Bildern_1860_155.png.

resurrection of the dead. "Judas," states the passage:

> took up a collection, man by man, to the amount of two thousand drachmas of silver, and sent it to Jerusalem to provide for a sin offering. In doing this he acted very well and honorably, taking account of the resurrection. For if he were not expecting that those who had fallen would rise again, it would have been superfluous and foolish to pray for the dead. But if he was looking to the splendid reward that is laid up for those who fall asleep in godliness, it was a holy and pious thought. Therefore, he made atonement for the dead, that they might be delivered from their sin (2 Maccabees 43-45 *RSVCE*).

Bodily resurrection is also professed by the third brother of the seven martyred brothers who were mentioned previously. Courageously stretching forth his hands to his torturers, the brother says, "I got these from Heaven, and because of his laws I disdain them, and from him I hope to get them back again (2 Maccabees 7:11 *RSVCE*)."

The account of the martyrdom of the seven brothers along with their mother does not emphasize dying for political change but rather describes them dying for God's law with the hope of gaining eternal life and of rising from the dead. This emphasis on eternal life distinguishes the seven brothers' deaths from deaths of the sons of Mattathias who ruled Israel: Judas, Jonathan, and Simon. As men of faith these three sons died for political, earthly change. Each died in a political office while fighting against Greek oppression.

In addition, beginning with Jonathan, the Maccabees combined their political role with their roles as high priests (1 Maccabees 10:20), an office they politicized.[8] This priestly office was even further politicized, and consequently the heavenly end of the priesthood was even more deemphasized, by the Maccabees wearing, observes Bergsma and Pitre, "vestments and symbols of royalty (1 Maccabees 10:20, 62, 64)." Finally, add Bergsma and Pitre, the decision of the father Mattathias to fight with his sons on the Sabbath, a day that is to be dedicated to rest, coupled with Mattathias' order to execute Jewish people who did not follow the law (1 Maccabees 2:44-47) also highlights the political dimension of the Maccabees' resistance to Greek oppression.[9]

In reaction to the politicization of the priesthood and consequent diminishment of the priesthood's role as a heavenly sign, the New Testament cautiously uses the Greek term priest that is equivalent to the Hebrew word for priest, *kohen* (כֹּהֵן).[10] The New Testament almost exclusively uses the Greek word for priest and high priest when referring to priests of the Old Testament, such as Caiaphas the high priest (ἀρχιερεὺς *archiereus* - Matthew 26:62), and to Christ as the high

---

[8] "Zadok," jewishvirtualibrary.org, https://www.jewishvirtuallibrary.org/zadok. "But only in the early years of Simeon, Jonathan's successor, was the high priesthood irrevocably transferred from the Zadokites to the Hasmoneans. This seems to have given the appropriate occasion for the crystallization of the Dead Sea Sect (see, e.g., Cross). The sect probably originated with a group of priests deeply disturbed by prevalent trends, especially in the high priesthood. The Hasmoneans were considered usurpers and the sect maintained the exclusive right of the Zadokites to fill the high priestly office."

[9] Bergsma and Pitre, 521-522.

[10] "3548. kohen," bible.hub.com, https://biblehub.com/hebrew/3548.htm.

priest (ἀρχιερεὺς *archiereus*). When referring to those who are ordained into the new priesthood of Christ, the Greek word for priest (ἱερεύς, *hiereus*) is not used. Nor, points out Benedict XVI, are those ordained referred to as officials with a specific office.[11]

Instead, the Greek relational, personal terms of elder (*presbuteros*, πρεσβύτερος), overseer (*episkopos*, ἐπίσκοπος), and servant, (*diakonos*, διάκονος) are used. For this reason, adds Benedict XVI, the Catholic sacrament of the priesthood is called the Sacrament of Holy Orders and not the Sacrament of the Priesthood to emphasize the other-worldly order of Christ and His Mystical Body the Church that the Catholic priesthood is to sacramentally represent in this world.[12]

The most important of these relational terms is *diakonos*, servant. One example of the importance of the term *diakonos* is found in St. Paul writing. This term denotes not only a ministry but also defines

---

[11] Joseph Ratzinger, *The Meaning of Christian Brotherhood* (San Francisco: Ignatius Press, 1993), 61. – Find Page Number "It never calls the officials "priests," or the office "office". The Greek words for office (*arkhe, exousia, time, telos*) are not, for the New Testament, appropriate descriptions for the offices of the Church."

[12] Ratzinger, *The Meaning of Christian Brotherhood*, 61. – Find Page Number "One can in no way identify the New Testament office, which is in fact New Testament service, with the phenomenon of priesthood in other religions. It is by nature something totally different. That it resembles priesthood factually, purely as a phenomenon, does not derive from its nature, but from the fact that a perfect fulfillment of being in the world of concrete appearances always remains impossible. It comes from a breaking in of the individual element which is not of Christ. So it is that, to this day, the sixth sacrament is called, in the language of the Church, not *sacerdotium*, but *ordo*."

the essence of ministries referred to in the New Testament (overseer – *episkopos*, elder – *presbuteros* - elder, and *diakonos* - servant). In the following passage, St. Paul is using the term *diakonos* to describe the essence of his ministry as an overseer, *episkopos*:

> Now I rejoice in my sufferings for your sake, and in my flesh I complete what is lacking in Christ's afflictions for the sake of his body, that is, the church, of which I became a minister (*diakonos*) according to the divine office which was given to me for you, to make the word of God fully known, the mystery hidden for ages and generations but now made manifest to his saints (Colossians 1:24-26 *RSVCE*).

Elders, overseers, and "deacons" are all ordered to service and, consequently, essentially defined by service, service to Christ. As Benedict XVI explains:

> The special character of the Christian office emerges with particular clarity when we compare the Christian apostle with his direct parallels in the history of religion, the rabbi and the *theios anthropos* ("man of God") of the Greeks. Both the latter have their own authority, whereas the essential thing for an apostle is to be a servant of Christ and, like Christ, to live by the motto, "My teaching is not mine, but his who sent me" (Jn 7:16). Thus, the sense of mission for the rabbi and the "man of God" is an awareness of self; for the apostle it is an awareness of service. "The rabbi's pupil has the goal of becoming a master himself. But for Jesus' disciple, discipleship is not a beginning;

it is the fulfillment and destination of his life. He always remains a disciple."[13]

Due to the Catholic priesthood's service orientation, the priest's role as father is not to be understood in an authoritarian manner but rather is always to be informed by service. As Benedict XVI asserts, the priest's "fatherly office is a form of brotherly service, and nothing else."[14]

As a brother, the priest is to sacramentally serve his fellow brothers and sisters by representing God's fatherhood and thereby foster a community of brothers and sisters in Christ who care for one another in a personal manner and not so much in an institutional, bureaucratic manner. As Benedict XVI explains:

> [I]n the classical theology of the Church, the Eucharist has been seen not so much as the soul's meeting with Christ, but rather as the *concorporatio cum Christo*—as the Christians' becoming one in the one body of the Lord. A celebration of the Eucharist that is to be the source of brotherhood must both be inwardly recognized and performed as a sacrament of brotherhood and also externally appear to be such. The recognition that *ekklesia* (Church) and *adelphotes* (brotherhood) are the same thing, that the Church that fulfills herself in the celebration of the Eucharist is essentially a community of brothers, compels us to celebrate the Eucharist as a rite of brotherhood in responsory dialogue—and not to

---

[13] Ratzinger, 62.

[14] Ratzinger, 60-62.

> have a lonely hierarchy facing a group of laymen each one of whom is shut off in his own missal or other devotional book. The Eucharist must again become visibly the sacrament of brotherhood in order to be able to achieve its full, community-creating power.[15]

A Eucharistic assembly that worships as a fraternal gathering in which community is fostered due to recognizing our equality before God the Father is to inform parish life, and relations between parishes. In asserting the importance of a fraternal parish life Benedict XVI writes:

> This aim of making the parish community a true brotherhood ought to be taken very seriously. ...the actual experience of brotherhood for all the Christian members of a parish community can and, therefore, should become a primary goal. It would be a universal experience which transcended all barriers, of course, for in every parish there are men of different professions and often of different languages and nationalities. It is this universality which gives the parish a superior position to an organization based on any other community of interests. And the parishes ought to come to see one another as sisters, according to the words of John's second Epistle (5–13)—sisters who, in the fellowship of their faith and love, build up together the great unity of the Mother Church, the body of the Lord.[16]

[15] Ratzinger, 68-69.

[16] Ratzinger, 70.

One way that clarifies the importance of understanding priesthood (bishop, priest, and deacon) as primarily a form of brother service is to properly define the commonly used term hierarchy. As Benedict XVI explains and admonishes:

> The correct translation of this term is probably not 'sacred rule' but 'sacred origin'. The word *arche* can mean both things, origin and rule. But the likelier meaning is 'sacred origin'. In other words, it communicates itself in virtue of an origin, and the power of this origin, which is sacred, as it were the ever-new beginning of every generation in the Church. It doesn't live by the mere continuum of generations but by the presence of the ever-new source itself, which communicates itself unceasingly through the sacraments. That, I think, is an important, different way of looking at things: the category that corresponds to the priesthood is not that of rule. On the contrary, the priesthood has to be a conduit and a making present of a beginning and has to make itself available for this task. When priesthood, episcopacy, and papacy are understood essentially in terms of rule, then things are truly wrong and distorted.[17]

---

[17] Ratzinger, *Salt of the Earth*, trans. Adrian Walker (San Francisco: Ignatius Press, 1997), 190-191; Joseph Ratzinger, *Church, Ecumenism and Politics: New Endeavors in Ecclesiology* (San Francisco: Ignatius Press, 2008), 126-127. "'Hierarchy', we should recall here, does not mean 'sacred dominion', but rather 'sacred origin'. Hence hierarchical ministry is the safeguarding of an origin that is holy, not the making of arbitrary decrees and decisions. Hence the ecclesiastical teaching office, and ministry in the

The repeated struggles, even involving murder, in the books of Maccabees over who rules as high priest serves as reminder of what the priesthood looks like when it becomes distorted by a desire to dominate and rule rather than by a desire to serve even if this means dying for those served.

Although the ministry of the priest is not about "positioning oneself," writes Benedict XVI, but rather of taking on the role of "Christ Jesus, who, though he was in the form of God, did not count equality with God a thing to be grasped, but emptied himself, taking the form of a servant, being born in the likeness of men (Philippians 2:5-7 *RSVCE*)" "[u]fortunately" laments Benedict XVI:

> [M]any people today see the priesthood in this way: as a chance to "have a place at the table" and "to have something to say" about the Church. But that is not what it is about. If we look at the great priests, starting with the apostle Paul, down through the ages to Charles Borromeo, the Curé of Ars, and Saint Paul of the Cross, then we see that it is always about something quite different, namely, about just what Christ did, who once told us: "The last will be first" (Mt 20:16) , and who truly being the First , the living God, personally became the last among men so as to come to us all. Being a priest means again and again entering into this gesture of Jesus Christ, being for

---

Church in general, is not the kind of 'leadership' exercised by an enlightened ruler who is confident that he possesses a better faculty of reason and translates it into ordinances, while counting on the obedience of his subordinates, who have to accept his reason and its decisions as their divinely willed standard."

> all and with all, even desiring to be one of the last, so that the light of the living God might shine everywhere. And, of course, this is then very promising.[18]

A second way that aids in understanding the Catholic priesthood as brotherly service also deals with the commonly used word power as purified and elevated by how Christ exemplifies power. Typically, power is immediately associated in people's minds with, explains Benedict XVI, domination, lording it over others (Matthew 20:25 *RSVCE*). Jesus, though, reveals a power that is not of this world, since His power derives strength from humble obedience to the will of God the Father. Jesus's power is, in the words of Benedict XVI, "humble power,"[19] not the crushing power of domination, of imposing one's will over others. Although power is often abused in this world, Christ did not come to eliminate power but rather to redeem and transform power by revealing another way of defining power. Citing Romano Guardini, Benedict XVI writes:

> Romano Guardini has very beautifully described the positive content of the fundamental act of Jesus, his crucifixion and attendant exaltation, as it is portrayed in the hymn of Philippians: "Jesus' entire existence is the translation of power

---

[18] Benedict XVI, *Teaching and Learning the Love of God: Being a Priest Today with a preface by Pope Francis*, trans. Michael J. Miller (San Francisco: Ignatius Press, 2016), 302.

[19] Joseph Ratzinger, *A New Song for the Lord Faith in Christ and Liturgy Today*, trans. Martha M. Matesich (New York: The Crossroad Publishing Company, 1996), 42.

> into humility ... into obedience to the will of the Father. Obedience is not secondary for Jesus, but forms the core of his being…" For his power there is therefore "no limit coming from the outside, but only one from the inside…: the will of the Father freely accepted." It is a power that has such complete control over itself "that it is capable of renouncing itself."[20]

By focusing on the Greek term that the New Testament uses when referring to Jesus' power, Benedict XVI further clarifies why Jesus' power is determined by His obedient will to his heavenly Father. He explains:

> To express this power of Jesus, the New Testament uses not a word that denotes the power inherent in a person, an existing concrete power, but the word *exousia*, which in Greek means the right to do something or a right over something, a right that is itself grounded in the legal structure of a state. The word describes a possibility of action officially given to a person as authority, right, permission, or freedom. We are concerned here with a *conferred* power, which comes from a legal system, that is, from a form of justice. Hence, it is authority derived from underlying power, and for this reason it carries weight. It is power arising from obedience, a power grounded in an inner

[20] Joseph Ratzinger, *A New Song for the Lord Faith in Christ and Liturgy Today*, 42.

order for which one accepts the responsibility.[21]

Since the power priests receive in participating in Christ's one high priesthood is likewise given, conferred power and not something that is found within themselves their primary influence is not to be derived from their natural qualities As Benedict XVI states:

> That a youth group likes the assistant pastor better than the bishop is nothing out of the ordinary. But that this results in a confrontation between two ideas of the church is no longer normal. For if the assent to Christianity is no longer addressed to the whole of the Church, but only to its amiable representation in the person of the priest or lay leader, then such an assent is certainly built on sand – on someone speaking in his or her own name. The motivator's personal ability now counts more than the authority in which he or she stands. As a result, however – even if at first no one is conscious of it at all – authority is being replaced with power, power that has been given and must be returned through one's own ability. The structure of *exousia* about which we spoke in the first part has been abandoned, and as a consequence what is essential has been lost. What makes the Church real is not that there are likable people in her, which is really always desirable and will certainly always be the case as well. The reality is her *exousia*: she is given the power, the authority to speak words of salvation and to perform deeds of salvation

---

[21] Joseph Ratzinger, *A New Song for the Lord Faith in Christ and Liturgy Today*, 42.

> which humans need and can never achieve on their own. No one can usurp the "I" of Christ or the "I" of God. The priest speaks with this "I" when he says: "This is my body" and when he says "I forgive you your sins." It is not the priest who forgives them – that would not count for much – but God who forgives them, and this definitely changes everything. But what a shaking event it is that a human being is permitted to utter the "I" of God! The priest can do it only on the basis of that authority which the Lord has given his Church. Without this authority, he is nothing but a social worker. This is an honorable profession, but in the Church we are looking for higher hopes, which come from a greater power. It these words of authority are no longer spoken and if they no longer remain transparent so that their foundation is visible, then the human warmth of the small group is of little use. What is essential has been lost, and the group will become aware of this very soon.[22]

Since Jesus' priestly authority stems from his perfect obedience to his heavenly Father's will and, consequently, receives heavenly power from God the Father, all aspects of Jesus including his knowledge are formed by obedience and, hence, directed towards service, a service centered around love of God the Father and love of all that the Father has created, in particular human beings, made in God's image and likeness. Unlike the first Adam who divorced knowledge from service and power from obedience, in Jesus knowledge, truth, power, and obedience inform one another since they are integrated by loving

---

[22] Joseph Ratzinger, *A New Song for the Lord Faith in Christ and Liturgy Today*, 54.

service and, consequently, not in tension with one another. As Benedict XVI explains:

> Adam is looking for knowledge as power. He is not looking for knowledge to understand the language of being better or to listen more accurately and thus be able to obey more faithfully; instead he is seeking it because God's power has become suspicious and because he wants to counter it with equivalent power. He is He is seeking knowledge because he thinks that only in rebellion will humans be free. He himself wants to be a god, and by that he no longer understands having to listen, but only exercising power. Knowledge serves the purpose of taking hold, of dominating. It is purely functional, geared to use and domination. Such power does not entail responsibility, but is only being able and being in charge. Its nature appears to be nothing short of having no one over oneself and referring everything to oneself and one's own use so that power may become the "splendor of power."
>
> ... In the account of the Fall one sees what it looks like when one accepts Satan's offer of power. Power appears as the opposite of obedience and freedom as the opposite of responsibility; knowledge is separated from its ethical components and measured by the standard of conveying power. Without condemning science and technology, we still have to say that something of this fundamental attitude has found its way into the modern practice of seizing hold of nature. A quotation from Thomas Hobbes is quite typical of

> this attitude: "Knowing a thing means knowing what you can do with it when you have it." It should be clear that this does not represent the "dominion" over creation entrusted to humans by God (Gen. 1:28-30).[23]

Satan's disobedient, crushing, proud, violent power is the power of death. In contrast, Christ's power is the power of an obedient loving servant who perfectly revealed this humble heavenly power by dying out of love on the cross. In contrasting these two types of power, Benedict XVI writes:

> There is a type of power, the kind we are most familiar with, which opposes God and is interested only in not needing God any longer, indeed in eliminating him. The essence of such power consists in making mere objects and mere functions out of other things and other people and subjecting them to one's beck and call. Other things and other people are not looked upon as living realities in their own right to whose distinctiveness I must submit; they are dealt with as functions, that is, in the manner of a machine, as something dead.
>
> Hence, such power is ultimately the power of death, and it also inevitably pulls those who make use of it into the law of death and the dead. The law that such people force upon others becomes their own. Here God's word to Adam is really valid: If you eat of this fruit then you shall die (Gen. 2:17). It cannot

---

[23] Joseph Ratzinger, *A New Song for the Lord Faith in Christ and Liturgy Today*, 43-44.

be otherwise if power is understood as the opposite of obedience, for people are not the masters of being, even where they can dismantle it into large pieces and reassemble it like a machine. Notwithstanding, humans cannot live counter to being, and wherever they talk themselves into believing they can, they fall prey to the power of lies, that is, to the power of non-being, of the pretense of being and consequently to the power of death.

This power can of course be very tempting and make a strong impression. Its successes are only temporary, but this period can last a long time and dazzle someone who lives only for the moment. Yet this power is not the true and not the real power.

The power that is found in being itself is strong. Whoever is on its side has the upper hand. But the power of being is not one's own power; it is the power of the Creator. In faith, we know that the creator is not only truth but also love, and that the two cannot be separated. God has as much power in the world as truth and love. This would be a somewhat melancholy sentence if we were only to know that much of the world that we are able to grasp in the space of our own lives and experiences. But viewed from the new experience with God himself and with the world which God has given us in Jesus Christ, it is a sentence of triumphant hope. For now we can turn this sentence around: truth and love are identical with the power of God, since he not only has truth and love but is both of them. Thus, truth and love are the real, the ultimate power in the world.[24]

Yet another way that best explains why the Catholic priesthood is essentially brotherly service is the Catholic theology of martyrdom that builds upon the theology of martyrdom present in the books of Maccabees.

25

In Catholicism, Christ's death on the cross is the fulfillment of the various kinds of martyrdom present in Maccabees. With that said, Christ's martyrdom is much more like the martyrdom of the seven

---

[24] Joseph Ratzinger, *A New Song for the Lord Faith in Christ and Liturgy Today*, 44-45.

[25] Gustave Doré [Public domain], "*The Courage of a Mother*, one of Gustave Doré's illustrations for *La Grande Bible de Tours*, 1866," https://commons.wikimedia.org/wiki/File:150.The_Courage_of_a_Mother.jpg.

brothers and mother whose deaths do not have a noticeable political emphasis but rather are directed to the heavenly world to come. This is evident in Jesus' refusal to be made an earthly king by fleeing to the hills when people wanted "to force" Him to be king (John 6:15 *RSVCE*), and as appearing as a fulfillment of the conquering "Lion of the tribe of Judah (Revelation 5:5 *RSVCE*)" by appearing as an innocent little lamb slain for our sins (Revelation 5:6, cf. John 1:29).

Jesus Christ's martyrdom is not the martyrdom of a political revolutionary (that the Maccabees at times tend to resemble) explains Benedict XVI, but rather the martyrdom of one who chose to be politically powerless since His "kingship is not from the world (John 18:36 *RSVCE*)." In describing Jesus as the fulfillment of all martyrdoms and the Revelation of martyrdom in its purest form, Benedict XVI writes:

> When the shepherd of all humanity, the living God, himself became a lamb, he stood on the side of the lambs, with those who are downtrodden and killed… It is not power, but love that redeems us! This is God's sign: he himself is love… God, who became a lamb, tells us that the world is saved by the Crucified One, not by those who crucified him. The world is redeemed by the patience of God. It is destroyed by the impatience of man.[26]

---

[26] Benedict XVI, *Day by Day with Pope Benedict XVI*, ed. Peter John Cameron (San Francisco: Ignatius Press, 2006), 136.

Section Questions

1. What two Catholic doctrines concerning our bodies and creation are contained in the narration of the seven brothers' martyrdom in the second book of Maccabees?

2. How can the New Testament very cautious use of the Greek term for priest which is a translation of the Hebrew term for priest be explained by the Maccabees approach to the priesthood? In your response include the following: Kohen, Archiereus, Presbuteros, Episkopos, Diakonos, Politics, Power

3. How does Jesus death on the Cross resemble the 7 brothers' deaths and less the 3 Maccabean brothers' deaths? Include in your answer the following: Martyrdom, Lamb, Crowned as King

www.ingramcontent.com/pod-product-compliance
Lightning Source LLC
Chambersburg PA
CBHW031429270326
41930CB00007B/632

* 9 7 8 1 9 5 2 4 6 4 2 7 0 *